The Mind of Christ

Revelations and Contemplations for Edification (and Conviction)

Olatunde Howard

Order this book online at www.trafford.com
or email orders@trafford.com

Most Trafford titles are also available at major online book retailers.

Note for Librarians: A cataloguing record for this book is available from Library
and Archives Canada at www.collectionscanada.ca/amicus/index-e.html

Printed in Victoria, BC, Canada.

ISBN: 978-1-4269-0220-8 (soft)
ISBN: 978-1-4269-0222-2 (ebok)

*Our mission is to efficiently provide the world's finest, most comprehensive
book publishing service, enabling every author to experience success.
To find out how to publish your book, your way, and have it available
worldwide, visit us online at www.trafford.com*

Trafford rev. 8/25/2009

www.trafford.com

North America & international
toll-free: 1 888 232 4444 (USA & Canada)
phone: 250 383 6864 ♦ fax: 812 355 4082

1

Table of Contents

Introduction 2-16
Preface 17-18
The Elementary Principles of Christ 19-29
Sin and Imagination 30-42
The Causes of Sin 43-50
Resistance 51-55
Binding Demons 56-67
The Fruit of the Spirit 68-80
Power 81-92
Christian Emotion 93-122
Impatience 123-125
Perpetual Arousal 126-130
The Praiseworthy Woman 131-137
Reflections on Corrections 138-141
Loitering 142-145
Appendix I 146-158
Appendix II 159-161

Introduction

In my experience, Americans usually introduce themselves indirectly, if at all; after "ice breakers" or small talk, or usually at the end of an icebreaker or small talk. Our society does not focus on clear, direct beginnings or endings. TV shows and movies reveal this.

For example: A business meeting is about to begin between two women who have never met. This meeting begins their work relationship. The first woman is looking out of a window in a previously appointed meeting area. The second woman enters and says, "Beautiful view isn't it?" The first woman says, "It sure is. I've never seen anything like it." "Don't get used to it. All new people are put in the offices with no windows. I'm Mrs. Such and Such. And you are…?"

Notice the "and you are?" The first woman isn't even given the ability to state her identity in a full sentence of her own. She states her identity as a completion of the second woman's sentence.

This should not be so with believers because we have no game to play with each other, no profiling agenda to see whom we are "up against." We are brothers and sisters, allies, friends. Our introduction should be direct. It should start with our names, our testimonies, and our ministry/divine destiny. Therefore, I will introduce myself to you in this way, telling you directly who I am and to whom I am writing.

I am Olatunde, which means "honor comes again." I am a son of God through faith in Christ Jesus, the Lord. I write to those who believe that Jesus died for our sins, rose from the dead, ascended into heaven, and will return for the sons and daughters of God. I will give you my testimony, to the best of my memory and understanding of it. This does not mean I don't want nonbelievers to read these words. It means that my assumptions will be those of a believer in Christ. In the appendix I will give these assumptions for those who do not yet believe, and if you, the one now reading, are interested. I hope after reading the appendix, if you are an unbeliever, you will become a believer. Amen.

I give my testimony in six phases because I believe it happened in six phases. After my testimony, I will give you my ministry, or my calling and purpose in life, which this writing is a part of.

1. *God with me*

From my earliest memory, from childhood, God drew me to Himself, and God was with me. I remember seeing a "vision" of myself as a baby, descending from the sky, from the sun, and then being held by my mother as my grandmother looked upon us both. We were in my grandmother's house, where my life began.

According to my mother, neither she nor my father were the influence in my life towards God, though of course they had a part in God's plan. It was not my upbringing or any human example given throughout my life. It was God Himself giving me an interest in Him. My grandmother's red children's Bible "stood out to me." It was not the color of the Bible, because the Bible seemed old and the color dingy. It was not a beautiful Bible. The pictures, to a certain extent, were frightening, like nightmarish paintings. But I was drawn to this book and its pictures. I don't remember anyone ever reading this Bible to me.

Then, at this same age, I remember two women in the neighborhood that conducted a children's Bible activity time. There were games and prizes. But these did not interest me, and I was aware that the "treats" were not my focus. What drew me was the Bible, or more specifically, the One spoken of in the Bible. These women sang this song, "Seek ye first the Kingdom of God," which was music put to Matthew 6:33. To this day I remember their voices singing this song. I remember how they ended the song, singing/saying the verse number, and how the rhythm of the song's ending didn't quite fit. This was the first glimpse I had of my musical gift. But this was also the very first time I was introduced to Jesus.

I attended church with my dad and my mom, but this made very little impact on me. I was "baptized" at about the age of six, which meant nothing to me; because I had no idea what I was doing and I was mainly scared I would drown. Church seemed boring most of the time. I thought it boring and needlessly emotional, with the traditional southern preaching that started "ok." but ended in the predictable "hooping and hollering." But before the southern black preacher drama, when the text was being explained in a somewhat normal voice, the word of God, again, unexplainably, interested me.

Though I was asked once if I believed that Jesus was the Son of God and that He died for my sins, and though I answered "yes," I didn't hear the gospel until I was 17. I had many spiritual experiences, some with angels, and some with demons. I had a prayer supernaturally answered. But I had never fully been told the good news until I was in high school.

All I wanted was a girlfriend to hold hands with on band trips.

Intimacy.

A best friend and potential wife from my youth.

It seemed that God answered me. I knew her from elementary school. She was my high school sweetheart. And her stepfather was a pastor. He didn't "hoop and holler," but taught scripture, verse by verse. One day in Bible study he said these words, "Did you know that by believing in Jesus you have a guarantee of going to heaven?" I had never heard this in my entire life, not at any church service I had gone to. I experienced the mental sensation of a "light bulb" coming on in my mind. This to me was good news indeed. I felt I wanted to tell everyone, literally everyone. I wanted to open the phone book and tell everyone. I told many of my high school friends. I believed I was going to be a "missionary." I even believed I was "called" to do so, though I didn't even know what a missionary was. I just told God I wanted to give my life to Him in service.

I asked Him what He wanted me to do and the word "missionary" came into my mind. Again, I didn't know what it meant, but I agreed. And sure enough, a youth minister asked me if I wanted to go on a short-term mission's trip with him to Israel. I accepted and God provided for me to go. But before this, though God was with me, something was missing.

2. God in me

As I said earlier, I desperately wanted intimacy. I wanted to be married, even from a young age. I was a virgin. I "struggled" with temptation from my girlfriend. One night was particularly difficult, and I came close to losing my virginity. This was the second time we had gotten this close. The more we sinned physically, the more guilty and convicted I felt. But she seemed not to be bothered at all. In our first physical encounter, she initiated physical contact with me. I moved her hand. She seemed embarrassed, so I let her touch me. I do not write as though I was a victim, but I can say that I did not initiate the physical relationship with her.

On this second night of sin, I felt like killing myself. I feared I had lost my virginity. Then suddenly, alone, in the dark, in my room, for no reason that I can think of, I said these words, "I believe that Jesus Christ is the Son of God and that He died for my sins." I felt peace cover me like an invisible blanket, and I no longer wanted to kill myself. I met a woman after this whom I believe was a prophetess. I met her at a teenaged pregnancy clinic. I went there because I wanted to know if I was still a virgin. She told me not to worry about that, but to know that God had a powerful destiny awaiting me, and that I needed to leave my girlfriend or things would only get worse.

I didn't know how to leave my girlfriend, and I really didn't want to, so I asked God to get me out of the relationship. Sure enough, my girlfriend came to me out of the blue and broke up with me. I couldn't believe it. It's not that I thought this impossible for her, but she didn't seem to want to end our relationship before, and I didn't have the nerve or the true desire to do it either. This was a miracle to me.

But, like a fool, when she later asked if we could be together again, I said yes, and things did get worse, meaning we continued to be physical, though without me losing my virginity.

Barely.

I had to break up with her right before the prom. This was heart breaking for her. We had been together since my junior year. We went to the junior prom together. I was voted prom king, which for my girlfriend would have been like a high school dream come true: to go to the prom on the arm of the prom king. I hated breaking up with her in this way, and I wish I had not hurt her so. But we had come very close to intercourse on my junior prom night, and I felt that if we went to the Senior Prom together, with all the sexuality that is assumed on prom night, I would have certainly lost my virginity.

I was not only voted prom king, but I was also voted the speaker for the graduation ceremony. I chose this as my topic: "The Ultimate Graduation Gift." And what was this gift? It was none other than the gift of salvation. Indeed, I would share the gospel with a coliseum full of people. I planned the gospel presentation based upon what I learned from my pastor. This presentation had two components:

A. The question.

B. The "Roman's road, "

The Roman's road, for anyone who may not know, is a series of verses from Paul's letter to the Romans that can be used to share the way of salvation:

-There is none righteous, no not one.

-All have sinned and fallen short of the glory of God.

-The wages of sin is death, but the gift of God is eternal life through Jesus Christ our Lord.

-For God commended His love to us in that while we were sinners, Jesus died for our sins.

-Therefore, whoever calls on the name of the Lord shall be saved.

Before walking someone who is unsaved down this road one could ask this question:

"If you were to die right now, and you stood at the gates of heaven, and God asked you, 'Why should I let you into heaven?' what would you say?"

There is one and only one right answer to this question:

"I believe that Jesus died for my sins and rose from the dead."

If one adds to this, subtracts from this, or negates this, one does not know the way of salvation.

So I decided to share the gospel using this method, giving a brief introduction that related to different kinds of graduation gifts, and then focusing on the best graduation gift, the best way to start one's adult life: accepting the gift of salvation and a new life, a new beginning.

The day came. The moment to speak came. I looked at the crowd and took a breath. And then it happened.

I felt an invisible "liquid" fall on my head. I literally, physically, tangibly felt this, just as I had literally and tangibly felt an invisible blanket cover on the night of sin. I came to know later what this was.

It was the "anointing." It was the Holy Spirit "falling upon me." In the Bible, this "anointing" took place with Kings who received power to rule Israel. Prophets also received an anointing. Oil poured upon the head to inaugurate a commission.

The Holy Spirit was with me.

The Holy Spirit was in me.

3. Now the Holy Spirit was upon me, empowering me to preach the gospel in power.

And in power I preached, and all who were there heard God.

My testimony has always been difficult for me because it didn't seem simple. I didn't simply hear the gospel, believe it, receive the Spirit, and begin ministry. But I thank God for scripture, because I do see a parallel in scripture to my experience thus far in these three phases.

Jesus said that the Spirit was with the apostles and would be in them. So when he sent them out, the Spirit was with them, but could not be in them until after He rose from the dead. When He rose, He breathed upon them and said, "Receive the Holy Spirit." Clearly the Spirit was in them at this point but not "upon" them, because He said that they would "receive power when the Holy Spirit came upon them." So, the Spirit was with them before the resurrection, in them immediately after the resurrection, and would be upon them after the ascension, on the day of Pentecost.

So far, I had these three experiences. But three more remained.

I learned Bible Study methods by Howard Hendricks, an author and a professor at Dallas Theological Seminary. I learned these methods from the pastor who was the stepfather of my high school sweet heart. The purpose, for me, in learning this was that I considered scripture the means to the end of God talking to me directly. Howard Hendricks said that the fastest way to grow was to meditate on scripture. I found this to be true. And I believed that while I meditated upon scriptures, God would speak to me, interrupting my thoughts, just as He interrupted Peter's thoughts while he thought about the vision of the unclean animals. I was very aware of God's presence, His listening ear in my meditative prayer, but I did not yet know His voice.

Bible study methods became dead, the dead "letter." I became hungry. I desired "something else," but I didn't know what. I spoke to a brother in Christ that I highly respected one who lived a holy and powerful life. I asked him why the Christian life was so defeated and weak. He took me through the scriptures, knowing that if he didn't present chapter and verse to me, I would not listen. He showed me the necessity of being filled with the Spirit, and that one of the evidences of this was speaking in tongues.

I had experiences with tongues before, some positive, most negative. The positive ones came with my stepmother. I heard her one night speaking "another language." That's what it sounded like, not "gibberish," not "ecstatic utterances," but a language, fluent and free. But I knew that my stepmother was an uneducated woman, not having gone beyond high school, if that. She was intelligent, but "uneducated." I knew she hadn't studied or learned another language. I asked my older brother what she was doing. The reason I asked this was because there was a power and intrigue to what she did that went beyond someone simply speaking another language. There was "something about it." He told me she spoke in tongues. She was not emotional or out of control. She was doing this alone, in her room, on her bed, at night. She did this in a normal tone and medium volume. She wasn't drawing attention to herself.

That was the good experience of tongues. The bad experiences were the overly emotional and irrationally insane tongues where people sounded and acted crazy, speaking gibberish loudly, and running around the building, sometimes head first. Just as Paul warned, I thought them all to be mad! In addition to this, I experienced the phenomenon of someone trying to teach me/make me speak in tongues. This totally turned me off. I wanted no part of this "emotionalism." I wanted the objective word of God in Bible Study Methods. But my brother showed me scripture that I could not resist or refute with the Bible Study methods; instead, the methods affirmed them.

I never heard this brother speak in tongues, nor did I know that he did so. He never did so around me because he knew of my past experiences. I wasn't necessarily against tongues all together. I thought, "If it will help me be intimate with God, then I am open." But I saw no real way that it would do this. How could it?

Yet I wanted more than the dead letter. And my brother convinced me through scripture. So I did what he said:

I heard the word of God. I believed the word of God

I asked God by faith to fill me with His Spirit, and that it would be made evident in tongues, as had happened in the Book of Acts.

I thanked God by faith.

I took a breath.

I opened my mouth.

And I spoke a language that I didn't learn by imitation, association, or duplication; a language I did not understand with my mind.

4. The Spirit of God filled me, just as they were filled with the Spirit on the Day of Pentecost, and I spoke with another tongue as the Spirit gave me utterance.

Now my brother did not teach me about tongues, interpretation, prophecy, and testing the spirits. I learned some things through trial and error.

But I was filled with the Spirit, and experienced the Holy Spirit as actually in me and overflowing from me. My life changed from that day forward.

I just enjoyed the fact that I was experiencing a genuine supernatural spiritual experience. But one day, as I was "singing in the Spirit," English words came out of my mouth. Now remember, I knew nothing of prophecy and interpretation. These were the words:

"I am with you."

Now these words are not "deep," but I knew one thing: God had just spoken through my mouth. I knew it wasn't Satan or a demon because I had experienced demon possession, being possessed and witnessing one who was possessed. This was not a demon. And further more, later on I found a scripture in which an actual Old Testament prophet gives a prophecy to Israel. And guess what the prophecy was?

"Thus says the Lord: 'I am with you.'"

That was the prophecy!! God didn't say anything else through the prophet at that time. He just affirmed His presence with them in their obedience to Him.

I thought to myself, "This is a way that I can talk to God and Him to me." Now note again, I didn't know 2 Samuel 23, the last words of David, where he said, "the Spirit of the Lord spoke by me and His word was on my tongue. The Rock of Israel said; the God of Israel spoke to me." Note what David is saying. God spoke to David by speaking through him. God spoke to David through his own mouth. David prophesied, and the prophecy David spoke was to David himself. This is what happened and still happens to me.

Not long after this, I made this decision,

"I would only do what the Spirit told me to do."

5. The Spirit of God led me.

I experienced the Spirit literally leading me, bringing glory to Jesus and to God the Father, edifying believers, and convicting nonbelievers.

So, the Spirit was with me, in me, and upon me, filling me and leading me.

And here I am, at this moment, writing to you as an oracle, a minister or God's word.

6. The Spirit empowers as a minister of the word.   I speak according to the power of the Holy Spirit who is in me.

My anointing came at my high school graduation, but I did not know it then, nor did I experience the power of being anointed, at least consciously. There were times when I would speak with power, but I did not realize then what I do now. And what do I realize now? I know that every one who believes in the Lord has at least one spiritual gift. This gift is their ministry, and this ministry is their activity, as Paul said to the Corinthians. It is the calling of the believer, what the believer is supposed to be doing. And when the believer uses his or her gift, the Spirit is manifest. I use the gifts God gave me by the Spirit to write to you. I do not write from human wisdom or education, because that would not benefit you in knowing and being like God. Only the Spirit of God knows the thoughts of God. My desire is not merely to share my thoughts or opinions or imaginations. My desire is to share with you what God shares with me by revelation. I seek the mind of God and the heart of God, the mind of Christ. Only

God can reveal His heart and mind. Therefore, I depend upon His Spirit to do so. And what He shares with me, I share with you. I choose to be a faithful and true witness of the Lord Jesus by the Spirit who empowers me. Amen.

10/01/08 7:35 AM
I wrote to you concerning my testimony and how it seemed best understood to me in "phases." I have one more phase to write, the one I consider most important.

7. On September 19, 2008, my 35th birthday, I decreed that I would walk with God for the rest of my life, as Enoch walked with God from the time he was 65 until he was 365, and God took him so that he did not see death. Enoch had this testimony, that he pleased God. And he had this testimony by faith. Enoch was a man just as I am a man. I have faith. Therefore I have Enoch's testimony in Christ Jesus, and I walk with God as he did, by faith.

"When I was a child, I used to speak like a child, think like a child, reason like a child; when I became a man; I did away with childish things." I Corinthians 13:11

I am a man, the image and glory of God.
I reject passivity, accept responsibility, and bravely take my authority, seeking God's honor and glory.
I have a will to obey, the will of the Holy Spirit who is in me. I have a work to do, the work of a prophet king. I have a woman to love: Lucy, the wife God gave me.
This is my transcendent cause, that which I consider truly heroic, requiring bravery and sacrifice (worth fighting for and dying for), which I consider timeless and supremely meaningful (being the very purpose for which I and all men were created): that honor comes again to man, the image and glory of God.

"Those who honor Me I will honor, and those who despise Me will be lightly esteemed." I Samuel 2:30

I give supreme honor to the Lord Jesus Christ, the True Knight, the last Adam, the Son of Man, and the Second Man.

I give honor to my father and mother, for without them I would not exist.

In honor of My Father on Earth:
Edward Louis Howard is my father.

He was a protector, a lifeguard and a fireman. My mother met him by an act of his protection over her.

Some of the very best times of my life came at my father's house, where my brothers and I were free. We ate things that our mothers would have never let us. (Smile)

We shot firecrackers, rode motor cycles, rode our bikes all over Macon, Georgia, swam in deep water, burned milk cartons, stayed up all night, and went to the movies with our dad, the fireman, for free. He taught me and my brothers to love each other. He hated untruthfulness and uncleanliness. He loved to laugh. He still does.

In honor of Georgia Mae Ellis-Gary is my mother:
She is a teacher.

She provided my brother and me food, clothing, and shelter. She gave us wonderful birthdays and many magical Christmas times. She taught us to be polite and to respect our elders; to put our needs before our wants.

She told me that nothing was wrong with me, and prayed that God would give me godly men when I left for college, afraid of failure.

I remember the two times of my life when I felt most confused, most insecure, and most afraid:

A. When I was 13, in middle school.

I remember laying my head on my desk in school, feeling alone and uncertain of whom I was. It was not until I was in the band that I found my "niche," where I fit in, what I could do, who I was; a purpose.

B. When I was on my way to college, at 18.

I remember crying before my mother, afraid of inevitable failure. My mother sensed my need: a godly man to give me direction. She prayed this for me. I remember being in college and seeing the upper classmen, who seemed so secure and confident in whom they were. I envied them. Now I know I needed a man, my father, to show me how to be a man. I needed him at 13 and at 18. He didn't know how to lead me in this way. But God the Father helped me, and after many years gave me the answer to the most important question of my whole life: What does it mean to be a man?

I give honor to Sir Robert Lewis, my brother in the Lord, who taught me manhood and knighthood.

I give honor to Pastor Jack Hayford, who taught me to draw near to God through worship that He might draw near to me in response to my worship.

In Christ I am new, a knight, one with God. He gave me my new identity and intimacy with God.

When He died, I died.

When He rose, I rose.

When He ascended, I ascended.

When I confessed Jesus as the Christ who died for my sins, on a night when I wanted to die for my sins, on a night in the year 1992, I felt peace cover me like a blanket.

And in college, I received a name from God that encompassed my identity and destiny.

On that day, I became who I am; I became a man; I became a knight. God my Father gave me intimacy and my identity, my vision, my code, and my cause. Amen. Amen. Amen.

I pray for grace from God my Father, the perfect father, grace to be like Him to my sons and my daughters, to give to my children what my father and mother gave to me, and to give to them what my parents did not know how to give to me; to teach my sons to be like Christ, true men; and to model to my daughters true manhood, that they may have husbands who love them as Christ loved the church; who love them more than I do.

In Jesus name. Amen.

Preface

At times I have "thoughts." I think, then speak, and then write. These thoughts pour out of my mouth or flow through my fingers. At times my mind is filled with imaginations and contemplations. I need to speak and write. Need.

Therefore, I need someone to listen, someone who needs to hear or read. But what is this mutual need? I believe it is the need to edify and be edified.

There are many topics that I want to speak about and write about, many thoughts. Those who believe in Christ have the mind of Christ. I believe in Christ, thus I have the mind of Christ. Therefore I think the thoughts of Christ. These are the words I speak and write.

Now what about you, the one who listens; the one who reads? What do you want to hear or read? If just nice, interesting thoughts, I advise you not to read these words. If opinions and stimulating discussion, I advise the same. I don't want to stimulate you or interest you. I want to strengthen you spiritually.

Who are you? To whom do I write? I answered this in the introduction. But for now, know what leads me or motivates me to write.

My wife and others have said these words, "You should write that down. You should write a book." I love speaking and writing, and feel that I have so much in me at times that I must "get it out." This is how C.S. Lewis described his inclination to write. I am sure others who are called to write feel the same, though it may be varied in expression.

Ultimately, I feel a "burden" at times. I feel weight that must be lifted, lightened. When I speak or write, the weight is released. I believe God gives us all burdens in different directions. Some to speak, some to write, some to act, some to do two or all three of these. I believe God chooses readers and writers.   God connected you and me somehow.   In a very real sense, I was made for you and you for me, or God had us in mind when He made each of us; that our paths would cross in this very way.

Even if you read these words and decide not to read further, I pray that God will lead you from this sentence to the fulfillment of your destiny. Thank you for reading this far. I always feel as though I need a very real audience or listener or reader. So I address you as though we were in the same room, face to face. The good thing about speaking is the possibility of immediate feedback or dialogue. I prefer this. But for now, my job is to "know exactly what I want to say and to say exactly that," as C.S. Lewis said. So, what exactly do I want to say to you, the one who is reading right now?

I hope that God speaks through me to you.

That's it.

Love,

Olatunde

The Elementary Principles of Christ

The Foundations of:
1. Repentance from dead works and of
2. Faith toward God,
3. Of the doctrine of baptisms,
4. Of laying on of hands,
5. Of resurrection of the dead,
6. And of eternal judgment.

From these principles, these foundations, the believer is to move on to perfection, to maturity. But I know that for me these principles and these foundations were not laid. Therefore, I remind those who already have these foundations, and to those who do not have them, I give them to you as the Spirit gave them to the writer of Hebrews. The Spirit who was in him is in me and in you who believe in Christ. I simply say what the Spirit gives me according to the spiritual gifts in me for God's glory, according to my meditation upon Hebrews 6:1-2.

1. Repentance From Dead Works
The first word of ministry spoken by John the Baptist, the Lord Jesus Christ, and the Apostle Peter was this word:
REPENT.
Change your minds. Change the way you think. Stop thinking one way and start thinking in a completely different way, even the opposite way. Change your minds, and thus change your actions. Leave the old life, and embrace the new. Leave the kingdom of darkness and enter the kingdom of light. Renounce the antichrist and receive the Christ.
But more to the point of this verse stop doing "dead works." If we are to stop doing dead works, then we are to start doing "alive works." I will show the difference by moving to the next principle.

2. Faith Towards God

"You see then that a man is justified by works, and not by faith only." James 2:24

"For as the body without the spirit is dead, so faith without works is dead." James 2:26

Now notice James 2:26 above. The body is compared to faith, and works is compared to the spirit. The spirit animates the body. The spirit in a person is what animates the person, making the person alive. So, applying this to "dead works," and also to "dead faith," we see this truth:

Faith without works is dead. (Dead Faith)

And works without faith is dead. (Dead Works)

Faith is like a body. Works are like a spirit. Faith needs works like a body needs a spirit

Faith without works is like a dead body in a casket; a corpse.

Works without faith is like a ghost.

Both are incomplete.

So repentance from dead works means to stop doing things without first believing a promise of God; to stop actions apart from faith. And Paul said that actions without faith are acts of sin. What is faith? Faith is to hear the word of God, to receive it as true and trustworthy and good, and to act upon it. There is no conflict at all between faith and works (or works of faith.) The difference between works of faith and works of the law is this:

Works of faith do not seek to save or justify one's self by one's own merit.

Works of the law do seek to save or justify one's self by one's own merit.

Paul said it this way,

"Now to him who works, the wages are not counted as grace, but as debt. But to him who does not work, but believes *on him who justifies the ungodly, his faith is accounted as righteousness."*

You don't work for a birthday gift. The gift is given in appreciation and love, and is in no way earned because you didn't "earn" being born.

But you do work for wages agreed upon between you and your boss. You and your boss decide how much your time and energy is worth in dollars, what the "minimum wage" will be for the time you worked. If you agree to work 40 hours a week for 1 dollar an hour, then at the end of 40 hours you expect 40 dollars. You expect it. This is not given to you out of the goodness of the bosses' heart. Whether the boss likes you or not or whether you like the boss or not, you expect your 40 dollars.

However, it is not right to "expect" a gift; to obligate one to give you a gift based upon how good you are or how good your actions are. This would be a debt that you are owed.

Gifts are given freely.

Wages are debts.

Salvation is by God's grace (unmerited and undeserved favor) through faith (us receiving his favor) not of us or of our works; it is a gift from God; we have nothing to boast about, according to Paul.

But note what else Paul says, "For we are God's workmanship created in Christ Jesus to do good works which God prepared for us before hand."

So, works that are not dead are works that express faith and works that God prepared for us, not works that we prepare for ourselves in order to boast of our merit and earn our way into heaven.

Again, faith without works is dead, and works without faith are dead. I said works without faith is a "ghost," in that a human spirit without a body is a ghost, according to the analogy of the body without the spirit and faith without works. Yet I want to focus on the spirit as the life of the body. Without the spirit, there is no human life. And in the same way, according to the writer of Hebrews, inactive faith is lifeless or dead faith. God created the body before he breathed into it the breath of life. In the same way faith must precede works of faith; it must be the foundation of works of faith. But faith must be active to be real. We all know this intuitively. We all know that "actions speak louder than words." We all know that what a person says or does, especially in times of trouble and pressure, before one can edit words or actions, expresses what one "really believes." This is all James is saying.

For example, if I give you a toaster as a birthday gift, two "actions" usually follow the receiving of a gift, and thus this gift:

-Thanks or some verbal and/or nonverbal expression of appreciation

-The actual use of the gift

If you thanked me for the toaster, but never actually toasted any bread, then I   would not be certain that you really appreciated the gift.

Think of salvation like this gift, or any valued gift, as the most valuable gift you can think of.

Here are the possible responses:

-Absolute hostile rejection of the gift; throwing it away, tearing it up, etc.

-Passive rejection, meaning to simply not take the gift or not unwrap or open the gift

-Passive acceptance: to take the gift, say thank you, but not use it

- Active acceptance: to thank the giver and use the gift

We are to thank God for the gift of his Son and "use" the gift of His Son for the forgiveness of our sins and for reconciliation to God. If we accept Christ, we will not try to erase our own sins or do things to merit God's love and favor. We will genuinely thank God for saving us and live with him in appreciative love and honor both now and forever, having been forgiven, and having been given a second chance.

So, in conclusion, to "repent from dead works" is to stop every intention, thought, word, or action that does not have faith as its basis. Every intention, thought, word, and action should be based upon confidence in God's words, promised or commanded.   Having understood these first two principles, let us move on.

3.   The Doctrine of Baptisms
John came with a baptism of repentance, which fits the first two principles and the first two components of the commission given in the gospel of Mark:
"Go into the entire world and preach the gospel to every creature. He who believes and is baptized shall be saved. He who does not believe shall be condemned."
So, the "baptisms" of the faith are these:
The baptism of John with water
The baptism of Jesus with the Holy Spirit, and thus the Holy Spirit's baptism of each believer into the death, resurrection, and ascension of Christ, and into his body.
John's baptism was a baptism that prepared the way for the Lord, a baptism of repentance. This baptism was and is serious. It meant total departure from the society in which the Jew lived, excommunication from the synagogue, family, and community.   Before one could follow Christ, he had to acknowledge John as the voice crying in the wilderness, the forerunner and herald of Christ. Today, though John is in heaven, as we see with Jesus' first message and Peter's first message, repentance follows faith, and baptism follows repentance. These are still necessary today.
Yet the greater baptism was and is the baptism of Jesus with the Holy Spirit. This is the promise of the God the Father, the very promise of Abraham, the new covenant. This is God dwelling in us and walking among us. This is the

restoration of the fellowship Adam and Eve had in Eden, perhaps even greater! We were born of the Spirit just as Christ was. And we received the same Holy Spirit that Christ received. We received the same baptism that the Jewish believers received on the day of Pentecost; the same that Cornelius and his family received; the same that the 12 Ephesians received by the laying on of Paul's hands, which leads to the next elementary principle.

4.   The Laying On of Hands
The prophets of old and the apostles of the church, as representatives of God Himself, laid hands upon believers, blessing and commissioning them for God given tasks, endowing them with the Spirit Himself and with spiritual gifts, including healing the sick. Today we take "spiritual gift inventories," and read books on gifts, which are not necessarily bad in and of themselves. But our scriptural example is that of apostles, prophets, or elders laying hands on members of the body and sending them out, imparting to them their ministry and activity. Observe these examples from scripture:

Mark 5:22-23 One of the synagogue officials named Jairus came up, and Numbers 8:9-10 so you shall present the Levites before the tent of meeting. You shall also assemble the whole congregation of the sons of Israel, and present the Levites before the LORD; and the sons of Israel shall lay their hands on the Levites.

Numbers 27:18 so the LORD said to Moses, "Take Joshua the son of Nun, a man in whom is the Spirit, and lay your hand on him;

Deuteronomy 34:9 Now Joshua the son of Nun was filled with the spirit of wisdom, for Moses had laid his hands on him; and the sons of Israel listened to him and did as the LORD had commanded Moses.

Mark 5:22-23 One of the synagogue officials named Jairus came up, and on seeing Him, fell at His feet and implored Him earnestly, saying, "My little daughter is at the point of death; please come and lay Your hands on her, so that she will get well and live."

Acts 8:17 Then they began laying their hands on them, and they were receiving the Holy Spirit.

Acts 9:17 So Ananias departed and entered the house, and after laying his hands on him said, "Brother Saul, the Lord Jesus, who appeared to you on the road by which you were coming, has sent me so that you may regain your sight and be filled with the Holy Spirit."

Acts 13:3 Then, when they had fasted and prayed and laid their hands on them, they sent them away.

Acts 19:6 And when Paul had laid his hands upon them, the Holy Spirit came on them, and they began speaking with tongues and prophesying.

1 Timothy 4:14 Do not neglect the spiritual gift within you, which was bestowed on you through prophetic utterance with the laying on of hands by the presbytery.

2 Timothy 1:6 For this reason I remind you to kindle afresh the gift of God which is in you through the laying on of my hands.

Healing, commissioning/sending, and empowering with the very presence and power of the Holy Spirit came through the hands of apostles, prophets, and elders. Jesus commanded his first apostles to go into the entire world and make disciples of all the nations. This laying on of hands is the application of Christ's command. The one making disciples is to baptize the disciple in the name of the Father, the Son, and the Holy Spirit, teaching them to observe all that

Christ commanded them. Having done this, the one who disciples lay hands on his disciple, imparting the power and presence God gave the discipler to the one being discipled.

5.   The Resurrection of the Dead

The essence of the good news is the resurrection. Without it, there is no salvation, justification, sanctification, or hope. There is no forgiveness. There is no heaven. The naturalist would be right, and we the most pitiful people imaginable. The early church preached Christ resurrected as Lord.

Necklaces with crosses with a savior still hanging in agony are not the gospel. He rose! He is alive!! He was seen by the 12, by Peter, by more than 500 at once, by James, the brother of Jesus, by all the apostles, and finally by Paul. He was seen!! We do not believe a fable or myth. This happened historically, actually, factually, and literally.

Not only this, but because of this, we will rise. And even more than even this, we have the very power of the resurrection in us, by the Spirit of resurrection. We possess the very life of God, life that is eternal, invincible. Again, this is literal. We have new life, the same eternal life that we will possess in heaven; the same spirit we will possess forever.

And our life on earth in union with Christ, our freedom from sin, is based upon the truth that we died with Christ to sin and we rose with him to a new life in relationship to God. This began the moment we believed.

This is an elementary principle because it defines the kind or quality of life that is normal for a child of God, both now and forever. We are a new creation, born again. Both of these common scriptural phrases assume the reality of resurrection. Death is the very curse of Adam and Eve's sin. Yet we see the hope of resurrection in the crying out of Abel's blood from the ground to God. We see Enoch escaping death altogether, (along with Elijah hundreds of years later.) We see Noah and his family saved out of the water of the old world, which according to Peter is a type of baptism, which according to Paul is the spiritual reality of death and resurrection. We see Isaac figuratively called back from the dead. We see Jacob "born again" as Israel, and Joseph, thought dead, alive indeed. We see Moses, meant for death, delivered from death. We see the budding of Aaron's rod, life from a dead piece of wood. Over and over we see life from barren wombs.

Throughout scripture God gave glimpses of the salvation to come: eternal life. We will live forever. The dead in Christ will rise and the alive in Christ will never see death!! Hallelujah! Death is an enemy to be resisted, as Watchman Nee wisely and scripturally taught. We should not accept death if we have not fulfilled our mission. We should expect at least 70 years otherwise, according to Psalms 90, even 80 years in strength. And more than even these, we should expect to be caught up in the air alive with Christ. This is the helmet of the hope of salvation by which we resist Satan and his many distractions of hopelessness. He wants us to think that this world, this body, this life is all there is. But we know and preach and live differently. As John Bevere has said, we are to be "driven by eternity."

6.   Eternal Judgment

"I have hope in God that there will be a resurrection of the dead, both of the just and the unjust. This being so, I myself always strive to have a conscience without offense towards God and man." The apostle Paul

This verse assumes eternal judgment. Eternal judgment is, by definition, once and for all and forever, final. Whatever comes out of God's mouth on judgment day will be final. If punishment, it will be eternal. If reward, it will be eternal.

Eternal!!

Once and for all and forever!!

When I read this in one of John Bevere's books, it devastated me with the fear of God. No sin or self-gratification is worth eternal loss.

From that book on, I decided I would be perfectly pleasing in the sight of God for the Day of Judgment and that I would know that this is so in the present. I will not be talked out of it. Paul's striving to have a conscience without offense, his prayer for the Thessalonians that God would "sanctify them wholly and preserve their whole spirit, soul, and body BLAMELESS at the coming of the Lord," as well as the very words of Christ to the seven churches of Asia in the book of revelations, where he makes clear to them that "he knows their works," and that one church's works were not "perfect" before God, and that he would come to judge and reward us according to our works, motivates me to do the works of faith discussed earlier, not for salvation, which I already have by faith, but for rewards. Yet even salvation cannot be taken lightly or for granted, for those who deny Christ in word or life may be "blotted out of the lamb's book of life." Christ could not blot someone out of this book UNLESS THEY WERE IN IT IN THE FIRST PLACE. And we know that unbelievers are not written in the book of life, but in the other books of judgment that will be opened.

Therefore, this elementary principle, this "given" of the Christian faith, is a very serious matter. We live for the day Christ will come for us, but he comes to judge the living and the dead; and judgment begins with the house of God.

Take heed to these principles and make sure that they are established in your life. Be sure that you have indeed repented from dead works and have faith towards God, animated by works of faith. Be sure you have been baptized, having died to sin, the world, and the law. Be sure that you know the call of God upon your life, the gifts of God's Spirit in you, by the laying on of hands. Know the hope of resurrection and the focus of eternal judgment in the fear of

God. With this foundation laid, move on towards perfection, towards maturity. Let no one talk you out of this. Be ready when Christ our Lord and Savior returns. I pray that this will be so for you and me in the name of Jesus. Amen.

Sin and Imagination

What happened when Adam and Eve sinned? Or what changed in their "natures"? And thus, what is the nature of sin?

"And the man and his wife were both naked and were not ashamed."
"I was afraid because I was naked; so I hid myself."
"The serpent deceived me, and I ate."
"Because you have listened to the voice of your wife, and have eaten from the tree about which I commanded you, saying, 'You shall not eat from it'; Verses from Genesis Chapters 2 and 3

The origin and nature of sin.
-Listening to Satan, the prince of darkness, the liar, the father of lies. "Indeed, has God said, 'You shall not eat from any tree of the garden'?"
-Believing Satan, accepting his lies as truth, and the truth as lies. "You surely will not die! "For God knows that in the day you eat from it your eyes will be opened and you will be like God, knowing good and evil."
-Acting upon Satan's lie, disobeying God. When the woman saw that the tree was good for food, and that it was a delight to the eyes, and that the tree was desirable to make one wise, she took from its fruit and ate; and she gave also to her husband with her, and he ate.
-Self-consciousness. Then the eyes of both of them were opened, and they knew that they were naked;
-Shame/fear. "And they sewed fig leaves together and made themselves loin coverings." "I was afraid because I was naked; "
-Hiding. "So I hid myself"
In a word, I believe doubt is the nature of sin, doubting God and trusting in one's self, or in Satan, the god of self-

exaltation. This doubt yields self-consciousness, which ultimately results in fear and shame, which leads to hiding, or dishonesty.

So, to answer the questions that began this writing, Adam and Eve became self-consciously fearful and shameful when they exchanged their sinless nature, the nature of child like trust in God's word, for a sinful nature, a nature of distrust in God and trust in ones' self.

But why did Eve listen to Satan instead of God?

Why did Adam listen to Eve instead of God?

Both seemed to do what Paul said, to suppress the truth, the word of God, and exchange the suppressed truth for the lie, the word of Satan, worshipping the creature (Eve worshipping the serpent; Adam worshipping Eve) rather than their Creator.

It seems to me that the issue was and is allegiance or loyalty.

Eve gave her trust and allegiance and loyalty to the serpent, and not to Adam or God. She neither consulted Adam or God before she ate. She considered the tree of the knowledge of good and evil for and by herself.

"When the woman saw that the tree was good for food, and that it was a delight to the eyes, and that the tree was desirable to make one wise, she took from its fruit and ate; and she gave also to her husband with her, and he ate."

"We walk by faith, not by sight."

Faith in God's word, not by faith in our own senses

It all began with entertaining the serpent, rather than subduing the serpent under her authority, correcting it for questioning her concerning the word of her and its Creator. She should have said something like this:

"Who are you to ask me what God said? What is it to you? What has the Creator said to you? Give an account of yourself to me, serpent, for it is you who owes an explanation to me. It is you who are to answer my questions and not me to answer yours. "

Thus the very first deception of Satan to man is the assumption of his own authority; his "right" to question both God and man; his "right" to an explanation of God's revelation. Who is he to come to Eve? Who is he? Where has he come from and where is he going? As God questioned Satan in the story of Job, so should we. We owe him no attention or explanation.

The deception of rebellion is the first sin; the creation's self exaltation and the Creator's humiliation and negation.

Eve's thoughts about the fruit: Good (to eat), a delight (to the eyes), desirable (to make [one(s) self] wise/ [like God, knowing good and evil])

Satan's sinful beginning: Uplifted heart because of his beauty

Corrupted by reason of his splendor

And Jesus said to them, "I was watching Satan fall from heaven like lightning."

"I will give thanks to you, for I am fearfully and wonderfully made; Wonderful are your works, and my soul knows it very well." King David

David acknowledged, thanked, and worshipped the Creator for creating him. Satan did not.

Satan looked upon his own beauty and splendor. Here to me is the "mystery of iniquity." Yet God assures me that there really is no mystery.

Consciousness and free will assume and reveal the possibility of iniquity, the ability of iniquity without the liberty of iniquity.

In other words, man is able to sin, but he is not free to sin. Man was able to eat from the tree of the knowledge of good and evil, but God did not give him freedom to do so, though he did have freedom to eat from the tree of life. He lost this freedom to eat from the tree of life after he fell, and he also lost the ability, for God had a cherub with a flaming sword to guard the tree, which means if the man tried to eat from this tree, the cherub would kill him. Again, he was able to try, but not free, and he was neither free to succeed in eating from it nor able to succeed in eating from it.

Lucifer knew God. Lucifer knew himself as not God. He possessed perfect beauty and complete wisdom. But he, being perfectly wise, must have known that his beauty was not the beauty of God, and his wisdom was not the wisdom of God.

He knew that he began, and thus his beauty and wisdom began; that they were limited, whereas God's beauty and wisdom are eternal and infinite; limitless.

What must have happened, therefore, for Lucifer to exalt himself in pride, and to thus sin against God? James tells us that God cannot be tempted to do evil and that he does not tempt anyone to do evil. So God did not tempt Lucifer to sin.

What was Lucifer's thought process that led to sin? What was Eve's? What was Adam's? What was mine? What was yours?

Thought: A baby boy comes to know that his mother is not an extension of his will, resulting in his fits and tantrums and other attempts to "will" her to action or reaction, to will her presence.

I remember a specific situation in my life in which I experienced, perhaps for the first time, the consciousness of freewill. There was a choice before me that no one compelled me to make or to not make. I thought through both options, to do or not to do, to say or not to say. I thought through the possible consequences of both options. I decided not to do one of the options, not to say what I could have said.

It seems to me that Lucifer had to have had the same kind of moment of truth concerning his beauty and his will. Somehow, he saw himself distinct from God, knew the option of self-worship or divine worship, the consequences of both options, and the means by which to act or not act.God or Lucifer. God or me. Which will it be?

This possibility is inevitable. If I am free, I can choose God or me. But again, the question is why I would choose me instead of God? Surely God is good, acceptable, and perfect in every way, infinitely more than I am.

But I believe God "lacks" one thing. He will not and cannot submit to me or live for me. If I am a sinner, and I want my will to be done like His will is done, then I want what I cannot have. If I want to be worshipped as God Himself is worshipped, to receive what is not rightfully or logically or desirably mine, then I want what I cannot ever have. I want to be what I am not, who I am not. I want to be God.

Now Lucifer only said that he would make himself LIKE the Most High. He didn't say he wanted to be God. But if he could of his own will make himself like God and exalt himself to the position of Most High, then he is indeed equal to God, and therefore, for all practical purposes, God Himself.

Now indeed, this, to me, makes sense, whether for myself, or for children, or for angels or for humans. It is even "logical," as well as, to a certain extent, "desirable." It is also, in a way, "doable." How so?

It is logical or makes sense in that we who are caused can understand non-causality and can, to a certain extent, participate in it. Our choices are Uncaused. God's choices are also uncaused. Of course, the difference is, God is uncreated, but we are created. Yet once God creates us, we are eternal, like a ray that goes on forever. So in this way, we are indeed like God.

It is desirable because God's sovereignty and power are attractive. Power and authority are attractive because they are divine. The authority of creatures is of divine origin as well. Self-rule or self-control in a person is very attractive, whereas the out of control nature of children, the insane, or the adult who simply does not control himself or herself is very unattractive. There is a certain sense in which the "freedom" of children is attractive, as well as the "freedom" of the insane. But this is only short lived, because this same "freedom" or boundarilessness is also expressed in lawlessness. And lawlessness is sin, the source of every conflict and the source of death itself.

And finally, making one's self like the Most High is, in a sense, doable because we have been given imagination. By this gift, we can be the center of our own little universe, in which all submit to our wills, even "God Himself," even the "God of Abraham, the God of Isaac, and the God of Jacob," even "YHWH/Jehovah." I put the names of God in quotes because of course He cannot be truly subdued in one's imagination. But one can deceive one's self in this very way.

I know this from experience. I have lived in my imagination, where I am king and all are my willing and loving slaves. But I have seen that the imaginary seeks to become reality. This is the source of all criminality.

Notice babies. They exist in their own little worlds where everyone bends to their will: daddy, mommy, brother and sister. If a baby can't sleep, then no one can sleep. If baby is miserable, everyone near baby is miserable.

Observe the insane. Usually the insane exist in a non-reality, their reality. They cannot "cope with reality." This is the same with any kind of addict. The drug or object of addiction is used to escape reality.

Thus the foundation of every sin is this deception: I am God, defining my own reality.

Note bad guys in movies and comic books. Who do they claim to be, or what kind of intelligence and power do they claim? Do they not claim omniscience and omnipotence? Note the seductress. How much power does she desire to claim over men? And how many men does she desire this power over? If one man ignores her, does he not become her obsession until she has his submission? Is her beauty now the power by which she receives worship and service? Does she not claim the status of "goddess," with the title of "woman" not being high enough?

Examples of statements and phrases that claim or imply deity:

"I made you!"
"I own you!"
"I am irresistible!"
"It is better to rule in hell than to serve in heaven!"
"I am the captain of my fate. I am the master of my soul."
"I AM (T-SHIRT)"
"In Papa we trust." (Sloppy Joe's is a bar in Key West, Florida that author Ernest Hemingway frequently visited. Hemingway knew the owner of the bar personally and influenced the naming and nature of the bar itself. Every year Sloppy Joe's hosts an Ernest Hemingway look-a-like contest. One of Hemingway's nicknames at the bar is "Papa." Sloppy Joe's has a saying during the Hemingway look alike contest: "In Papa we trust." This statement of course is a play on the American statement, "In God we trust.")

The truth, the whole truth, and nothing but the truth, so help me Mack." (Title of a Bernie Mac movie)

All of these examples point to one thing: the creature usurping the Creator's throne by usurping the supreme uniqueness of his identity.

Note these important truths:

1. A "sinful nature" was not necessary for Lucifer, the fallen angels, Eve, or Adam to sin.

2. The knowledge of the evil one was not necessary for Eve or Adam to yield to him or to resist him.

3. The knowledge of evil was not necessary for Adam and Eve to commit evil or resist evil.

These three truths are crucial.

Therefore, what is necessary to sin?

1. One must know the God as the Creator and rightful Owner and Master or all creation, knowing Him to be perfectly good, perfectly powerful, and perfectly wise, perfectly unique as the unborn, undying, unlimited one.

2. One must know His will, and based upon His character already mentioned, one must know that His will is good, acceptable, and perfect.

3. One must reject God and His will in place of one's self and one's own will, knowing full well that to accept His will is eternal life and to reject His will is eternal death; choosing to reject His will in spite of this knowledge.

Do you know God the Creator and Owner and Master of all that exists?

Do you know that He is perfectly unique, good, powerful, and perfectly wise, and that His will is by definition supreme?

Do you know that you rightly owe Him your very breath, which belongs to Him, and that all that you are, all that you have, and all that you do belongs to Him; that all comes from Him and is being sustained by Him?

You and I exist. God created us by His will, for His satisfaction.

He is our origin.

He is our destination.

He is our meaning.

He is our reason.

This is reality and truth. God is my master and I am His slave.

Does this offend you?

If I spoke of a man or woman, white or black or yellow, I could see it offending you, because no human owns another human. But God our Creator does in fact and indeed own us, define us, and determine our actions. This is good. This is heaven. To be what our Creator made us to be and to do what our Creator made us to do is indeed joy unspeakable. It is purpose and fulfillment eternal.

But to reject God is hell and the lake of fire. When the finite seeks to become infinite and to find infinite pleasure in other finite things, this creates the hole within us, the insatiable, unfulfillable desire, which is the fire of hell itself.

God is God.

You are not God.

I am not God.

I believe that the realization of imagination is the beginning or end of sin.

This is the first true option of submission or rebellion.

One can offer one's imagination to God, so that when He rules the imagination, He truly rules the person.

Or one can withhold one's imagination as the one place off limits to God.

Yet our hearts will be judged, our secret intentions and imaginations will be exposed.

-Lucifer said in his heart that he would make himself like the Most High. He was corrupted and lifted himself up in his heart because of his beauty and splendor.

-Eve saw and thought about the tree of knowledge.

God saw that "every intention of the thought of the heart of man was only evil all the time." For this reason, he destroyed man by the flood.

My Father in heaven,

Once and for all I repent. I confess that I have been my own God in my imagination, worshipping myself and seeking worship from everyone else in this domain. I have sinned against you, every intention and thought of my heart and imagination being only evil all the time. I deserve the same death as those who died in the flood. I deserve hell and the lake of fire forever, for I have broken all of your commandments. I have disbelieved you. I have dishonored you and disobeyed you. I have not feared and revered you. I have been evil, your enemy, and your adversary. I have hated you and been the worthy object of your hatred and displeasure and shame and dishonor. Please forgive me and pardon me and cleanse me of all my unrighteousness and sin by the blood of Jesus. Thank you. I repent. I turn from worshipping myself in my imagination and I turn to worshipping you alone. I give my imagination and my intention to you. Amen.

Final meditations:

-Liberty assumes ability but ability does not assume liberty.

Example:

My son goes out on a date by my permission. My giving him liberty to go assumes he has the ability to do so. I tell him to be back by 11:00 p.m. He has the ability to stay out until 4:00 a.m., but not the liberty. Herein lies the possibility of sin. My son considers his ability but not his liberty, which comes from my authority. He considers his will, which is to stay out, and not my will, which is for him to come home. This is what Lucifer, Adam, and Eve did.

-The desire for our own kingdom/space/time is experienced and epitomized in imagination. We want our own time, "me time." But Jesus did not have "me time." He was alone with God in prayer, or with people, meeting their needs.

The sinner wants the same autonomy that God the Father has, to be accountable to no one. To live for one's own pleasure.

Note what God said about people in the Tower of Babel passage:

"Now the whole earth used the same language and the same words. It came about as they journeyed east, that they found a plain in the land of Shinar and settled there. They said to one another, "Come, let us make bricks and burn them thoroughly." And they used brick for stone, and they used tar for mortar. They said, "Come, let us build for ourselves a city, and a tower whose top will

reach into heaven, and let us make for ourselves a name, otherwise we will be scattered abroad over the face of the whole earth." The LORD came down to see the city and the tower, which the sons of men had built. The LORD said, "Behold, they are one people, and they all have the same language. And this is what they began to do, and now nothing which they purpose to do, will be impossible for them."

With God all things are possible.

But Jesus also said, *"If you can believe, all things are possible to him who believes."*

The new age thinking seen in movies like the Matrix is attractive because there is truth to it. United faith among people is very powerful. Humans have been given limited ability to create reality; but it seems that the only limit is our faith, or the measure of faith that we have received. Some directors decide to make movies based upon the limitless possibilities he saw with computer technology. Indeed, movies seem to be ascending to levels never before thought possible. Disney seemed to understand this, as expressed in the song "Imagination," and the theme park attraction bearing the same name.

This limitless possibility is the attraction of the imagination used for self-gratification. It is the power behind animation, the limitless ability given to man and woman, especially to super heroes and heroines. These have uncanny power and beauty and sexuality. And these are without limit. In these the glory goes to man alone, and not to God who made him.

Imagination must be brought in to submission to God.

Self-centered imagination, I believe, is the root and expression and continuation of sin.

Note: Paul said that the love of money is A ROOT OF ALL KINDS OF EVIL. Based upon all that God has shown me, I can see how. All I have to do is look at what God saves us from and how we would be if he had not delivered us. Let's say a man's worshipped women. Now how could he experience in reality what he could only imagine in fantasy: a world where as many women as he wanted submitted to his every desire? Rap videos give the obvious answer: MONEY!! Money is the means by which he, in this society, can have WHATEVER he wants. Note the rappers, throwing money around like it is nothing. Note how the women are dressed in the videos, the clothes, the glamour, the money, the fame, and the jewelry. These women submit to AND OBEY these musicians. Prostitutes and strippers can all be had with money, to whatever extent, according to how much one is willing to pay. The more money one has, the more women he can get. Money is the means to the end of self-gratification and the fulfillment of imagination. What is imaginary becomes reality WITH MONEY!!

In conclusion:

Give your imagination to God. Let His kingdom come and His will be done in your imagination as it is in heaven. Note these verses:

"As a man thinks in his heart, so is he."

"Those who live according to the flesh set their minds on the things of the flesh. Those who live according to the Spirit set their minds on the things of the Spirit."

"Set your minds on things above, and not on things below."

"Do not be conformed to this world, but be transformed by the renewing of your mind."

"God will keep him in perfect peace whose mind is stayed on Him, because he trusts in Him."

"Whatsoever things are true, noble, just, pure, lovely, admirable, excellent, and praiseworthy, meditate on these things."

"You have the mind of Christ."

"Let this mind be in you which was also in Christ Jesus: the mind of perfect humble submission to the will of God."

"God has not given us a spirit of fear, but He has given unto us a spirit of power, a spirit of love, and a sound mind."

"Exhort the young men to be sober-minded."

These verses show this truth: the battle is in the mind, specifically the imagination. If your secret thoughts, intentions, and imaginations are pure, the secret person you are that no one but God sees and knows; the person that you are when you are alone, then you are not a hypocrite. Jesus said all things said and done in secret would be brought into the open.

I know that I fear dishonoring God's name, my name, my families name, the name of man, the name of authority, and the name of the body of Christ. My biggest fear when I was in sin was getting caught. But God is merciful and willing to forgive, forget, and make forgotten. But we must not take Him for granted when it comes to our imagination. What we think in secret will be revealed. If what we imagine is good, then we have no shame. But if our imagination is evil, then our entire life is evil, and we have reason to fear, unless we repent and forsake sinful imagination. If we repent, God will forgive us and cleanse us of our unrighteousness by the death of His Son.

God is love. Love keeps no record of wrongs. Therefore, God keeps no records of wrong. He separates our sins from us as far as the east is from the west and casts our sins into a sea of forgetfulness. He blots out our transgressions and remembers our sin no more. If this is what you need for your mind and imagination, ask Him, and He will give it.

I do pray that our imagination and mind will be pure and that we may have no shame in what we think in secret. In Jesus name I pray this for you and me. Amen.

43

The Causes of Sin

Satan: resisted
His kingdom of Temptations: overcome
The right eye and right hand of passion: cut off and cast
away; crucified; deliverance
Temptations
Irritations
Aggravations
Oppositions
Rebellions
Insubordination
Exhaustion
Every day, the Lord's name is taken in vain.
Every day, I resist the seductress.
When will this age of sin end?
When will we be finally rescued from our bodies of sin
And Satan and temptations and demons?
I must pluck out my right eye and cut off my right hand.
I must throw them away.
My old self was crucified with Christ.
My body of sin was done away with.
Destroyed.
Rendered inoperative.
Rendered powerless.
Unemployed.
I am no longer a slave of sin.
In consider myself dead to sin, the law, and this world of
temptation.
Unresponsive.
I owe nothing to the flesh, am under no obligation of
submission.
Neither TV nor movie nor commercial control me.
Not a bulletin board or magazine or web page

Not a woman
Not a man
My battle is not with man or woman.
Not with Flesh and blood
I battle the principalities and powers
Rulers of the darkness of this age
The spiritual hosts of wickedness in the heavenly places
Satan
Demons
They are the power behind sin and self-gratification
I am strong in the Lord and in the power of His might.
Immovable in my connection and submission to God the
Son
In submission to God
In resistance of the devil
Defending the victory Christ won for me on Calvary
Sin is no longer my master.
The law is no longer my husband.
 I died.
I rose.
I ascended.
I am one with God.
As it is with Christ, so it is with me.
This is history and reality.
What is the truth with which I gird my waist?
What is it right now?
What is the way out that God has made, that I might bear
The temptation in front of me?
Reading.
Writing.
Praying.
My mind focused on these.
Self-denial
Simply not allowing myself the pleasure of desire.
How much is will?

How much is grace?
Works animate faith, so that neither faith nor works are
dead.
Do I believe I am freed from sin and the law?
What does a free man do?
When my ancestors were "emancipated" by Lincoln,
what did they do?
Some of them never knew manhood or womanhood.
Where would they go?
They might as well stay on the plantation.
Satan would have me think this, that there is no other
reality but slavery.
But I am free.

Here it is.

*"Do you not know that to whom you present yourselves
slaves to obey you are that ones slaves, whom you obey?"*
*"Do not let sin reign in your mortal bodies, to gratify it in
its lusts."*
*"Do not present your members to sin as instruments or
weapons of unrighteousness."*
*"Present yourselves to God as one who has been brought
from death to life."*
*"Present the members of your body to Him as
instruments and weapons of righteousness."*

In these quotations, Paul tells the Romans that they are to
give their bodies and body parts to God just as they gave
them to Satan, to sinlessness as they gave them to sin. With
the same single-minded devotion and faith that we sinned,
we are to stop sinning and start serving.

Serving.
Serving God and man.
Serving is the opposite of sin, which is in essence, self

gratification.
Self-serving.
Instead of stealing, work and give.
Instead of fornication and adultery, marry.
Burn the idol.
Worship the invisible God.
Sin must be replaced with sinlessness.
Unrighteousness must be placed with righteousness.
This is repentance.
So I come back to what I said earlier.
When sin is in front of me, turn around, and focus
behind me.
If sin is inside, go outside.
If sin is outside, go inside.
Turn from an object of sin to an object of sinlessness.
Right now, where I work, sin is before me.
I can't fully look behind me, but I have two screens as
options.
The computer screen, on which I now type, or the TV
screen, where lust is being presented.
Where is the union of faith and works, works and faith?
What is the difference between resisting watching TV "in
my own strength," and resisting in God's strength?
I believe the difference is summed up in one word:

Prayer.

I pray, "God, help me by your Spirit, the Helper, to help
me be true to my new nature."
I thank God for delivering me from sin.
I then act upon faith in these truths.

The Muslim or Buddhist or New Age practitioner puts
total trust in self's ability to attain purity. The believer in
Christ does not. He or she trusts in Christ as Savior and

Deliverer. We believe that God kills the old person who was enslaved to sin and recreates a new person, free and holy. Now our responsibility is to believe and act upon belief.

> Straining puts trust in self.
> I pray.
> I believe.
> I act effortlessly.

If I am a new creation, with a new nature, then as easily as it came for me to sin, it should come just as easily for me to resist sin and serve God. Do I find this to be so?

> I believe I do.
> My conscience gives me no peace if I indulge my body.

The law of the Spirit in me sets me free from the law of sin in my body.
The inclination
My body is inclined to gratify itself.

But there is a higher more powerful law in my mind and on my heart, within my conscience, my spirit, that will not let me sin easily.

> I despise shame.

I fear God's dishonor, and the dishonor of His name, my name, and the names of the body, authority, and masculinity.

> I am the return of honor.
> Honor comes again.
> To dishonor God is to destroy myself.

Slavery
Property

Who now owns me, defines me, and commands me? The Holy Spirit within me is my Master, and I am his willing and loving slave.

Slavery.

"The white man" never owned my ancestry or me.
I belong to my Creator and Savior and Father.
I am free to serve Him.

The Israelites were not free to worship the One True God, the God of their fathers, the God of Abraham, the God of Isaac, and the God of Jacob.   Pharaoh refused to allow them to worship God alone, because Pharaoh considered himself a god, and God will not be part of an Egyptian pantheon of gods.   He will not share His glory with idols. But He does share His glory with man, for man is His glory, and woman is the glory of His glory.
The Hebrews had to leave Egypt. They had to separate.
So do I.
So do we.
Whatever it takes to serve Christ.
If I must pluck out an eye or cut off a hand, so be it.
If I must deny allegiance to father, mother, wife, children, and my own self, so be it.
If I must be rejected, suffer, and die, so be it.
If I must forsake all that I have, so be it.
The causes of sin must be renounced and removed forever. All bridges to sin must be burned, no matter how painful or inconvenient this is.
This is repentance.
This is being born again.

Turn from evil to good, from Satan to God, from this world to the next world, from the visible to the invisible, the temporal to the eternal.

God's will, from beginning to end, is good acceptable, and perfect. Scripture says, "Taste and see that the Lord is good." God gives us all things to enjoy, and all that is good and perfect comes from Him. He does not simply say, "You shall not commit adultery." He also says through the song of Solomon, "Let your fountain be blessed and rejoice in the wife of your youth. May her breast satisfy you at all times, may you be intoxicated by her love always. Why be intoxicated by the embrace of and adulteress?" Paul again says that man and woman should marry and not burn in desire, and once married, they should not deprive one another except by mutual consent for a time of fasting and prayer. And after this time, they should immediately come together again (sexually) so that the devil will not tempt them. Satan is the one who tempts and teases and taunts and defrauds, promising and not fulfilling. God does not and cannot tempt men and women to sin. God has delights for us that we cannot imagine nor contain in these present bodies, the first and foremost and supreme delight being God Himself.

Christ, who died for our sin and died to our sin, has dealt with the causes of sin. In union with Him, we are free from sin and slaves of God, no longer owned or controlled by sin, but owned and governed by God's Spirit. Where the Spirit of the Lord is, there is liberty. In the Spirit there is righteousness, peace, and joy. In God's presence, there is complete joy and eternal pleasure. What created thing or being can give you or me this guarantee of satisfaction?

Jesus said, "I am the bread and water of life" and that the one who comes to Him will never hunger nor thirst. This is a promise of satisfaction. The causes of sin and enticements of temptation all promise satisfaction and bliss. You and I know this to be deception.   We know the disillusionment of trying to find happiness and being let down by people and jobs and vacations and gifts. The thrill is so short lived. The thrill of sin always is. But the satisfaction God gives is real and meaningful. He Himself is satisfied with us, which alone is heaven. And not only does He smile upon us when we believe in Him and act on this belief, but He gives us the privilege of satisfying others, serving as well as being served. He gives us gifts and talents and abilities that no one else has. He makes us solutions to problems and answers to questions. We are the fulfillment of needs and desires in others. We are significant and necessary. God has honored us with all of this. God is indeed good.

So, if you "struggle" with sins and vices, know that Satan is trying to keep you from seeing the truth of God's goodness and blessing. The devil hides the fact that God does not withhold good things from us, but wants us to experience goodness to the fullest extent. He is goodness to the fullest extent. And when we know this, supremely adoring our Creator, then we will appreciate His creation and enjoy it without worshipping it.

I encourage you; seek out the cause of the sins in your life, if there is any sin in your life. The cause is some single deception; something you believe about God that is a lie. Ask the Holy Spirit, the Spirit of truth, to reveal this lie and replace it with truth. Jesus said whoever abides in His word is a true disciple, and this one will know the truth, and the truth will set this one free. So clearly, bondage comes from lies, and liberation comes from truth. God's word is truth. God's Spirit is truth. God's Son is the way, the truth, and the life. And the freedom that Christ spoke of was none other than freedom from sinning. This is what He said to the Hebrews in the gospel of John. Christ came to set us free from sinning, from addictions and obsessions with creation. I pray that you and I may be free indeed.

51

Resistance

You and I have an enemy.
He is invisible, intangible, and inaudible, but very real.
He is a spirit, an evil spirit.
He has mind, emotion, and will.
He is very powerful, but not all-powerful.
He is very wise, but not omniscient.
He is completely evil and personally against you.
He wants to steal from you love, joy, peace, patience,
kindness, goodness, faithfulness, gentleness, self-control,
and all that is good and beautiful.
He hates God and he hates you personally.
His name is Satan, the accuser, and the slanderer.
He is your adversary, the devil.

The scripture says,

"Be sober and self-controlled. Be watchful. Your adversary, the devil, walks around like a roaring lion, seeking whom he may devour. Withstand him steadfast in your faith, knowing that your brothers who are in the world are undergoing the same sufferings." I Peter 5:8-9

Self-control is necessary for the very reason that he is a spirit, invisible and intangible, physically undetectable, in addition to the fact that he is a deceiver and liar, the father of lies. He is thousands of years old, having watched and learned about humanity. His plans are generational and familial. He has one goal: to be worshipped as God by man and woman. He is perfect in wisdom, having been wise as a former angelic being, Lucifer. Yet his wisdom is corrupted by pride, and is more akin to cunning and shrewdness.
Because he is not a physical being, it is easy for him to inject thoughts and emotions into an unaware person. If you

are not actively controlling your mind and will, and you just kind of "go with the flow" of your surroundings, letting thoughts go unchecked and unchallenged, accepting every emotion without question, then you can easily be deceived and controlled by Satan. Thus you and I need to actively control our minds and wills at all times.

For example, say you wake up in the morning, having had a good night's sleep. Your body is healthy and you are not against anyone nor are you aware of anyone who is against you. In other words, when you went to bed, all was well. Yet you wake up "on the wrong side of the bed." You are in a bad mood. Mad. But why? No one has yet said or done anything to you for you to be mad about. No person has knowingly or willingly hurt or offended or neglected you. But you are mad nonetheless. If you have been in the habit of passivity in mind and will, then you do not investigate this emotion, but passively accept it and go with it. Then, "from no where" you get this "thought":

"I think I might be bipolar."

You don't really know what it means to be bipolar or the symptoms. Yet you accept this as well. You greet your husband or wife or children or friend by saying, "I think I'm bipolar." Having agreed with a demon, you give him complete permission to bring about so called symptoms of bipolarity and a few other symptoms that have nothing with that diagnosis. The demon has you, and you don't know it. You don't know you have an enemy, a lying adversary bent on destroying God's purpose in your life.

I can't emphasize this enough. It is a real, personal, specific being that is really and truly against you, the one who is reading these words right now.

Some say you shouldn't "look for a demon under every rock," that you shouldn't "focus on the enemy." If by "look under every rock for a demon" one means, "don't be undiscerning, unwise, or wrongly diagnose situations as demonic," this is true. Every situation is not instigated by a demon. Much of what we do we bring on ourselves.

And if one means by "focusing on the enemy" that one's focus or meaning in life should not come from studying the enemy, this is also true. Whether we eat or drink or whatever we do, we do it all for the glory of God.

Yet we are at war, for Paul says that the "weapons of our warfare are not of this world." Paul also says we are to "stand against the wiles of the devil." Of course the goal of every just or godly war is victory, liberty, and glory. But who does not actively look for or "focus" on an enemy in war? It is to our best interest to be aware of the enemy's presence so as not to be attacked by surprise. We look for him. We focus on attacking and defending. Until the war is over, we do think about where our enemy is and what he is planning and doing. We don't live to fight, nor do we fight to live. The victory is won in Christ already. We resist for the purpose of maintaining the victory Jesus already won.

He deceives our minds if we are not self-controlled, actively focusing our minds on truth.

He ambushes us if we are not watchful.

And what do we watch for?

On one hand, the enemy is subtle, crafty, hard to detect, posing as an angel of light, a messenger of truth. He hides and disguises his lies.

Deception

On the other hand, he is the enemy of God. Therefore, whenever God's will is being carried out wisely and unambiguously, expect opposition from the enemy. In other words, my job and yours in relation to our enemy is to know the mind and will of God. When we know his mind and will, as Ravi Zacharias' has said, anything that "distracts, diminishes, or destroys the goal" of God is from the enemy.

Now this assumes that we ourselves aren't doing things that distract, diminish, and destroy the goal of God. This is where blaming the devil comes in. We should never make his plans easy to fulfill.

Assuming we have not aided the enemy, when we find something "just happens" to get in the way of us doing or saying exactly what God would have us to do or say, then by definition we have found the enemy attempting to stop us.

Rebellion.

God says to Adam and Eve, "If you eat from the tree of knowledge, you will surely die."

Satan says to Eve, "If you eat from the tree of knowledge, you will not surely die."

God says about Job, "Job is blameless and upright, fears God and shuns evil."

Satan says about Job, "He doesn't really fear you. (My paraphrase)

God says about Jesus, "This is beloved Son."

Satan says about Jesus, "If you are the Son of God..."

Whatever God says, Satan opposes, either by adding to, subtracting from, or negating God's word. The devil seeks to unsay what God says and undo what God does.

Therefore the key is the knowledge of the truth and submission to the will of God, believing only the mind and will of God.

This faith and submission towards God must be active.

And this resistance of the devils manipulations and lies must be active.

Who are you?
Who is God?
Who is your enemy?
These three truths must remain clear.

You are a child of God through faith in Christ Jesus, Your Creator, Lord, and Savior.

Your enemy is Satan and his army of demons, invisible, spiritual, yet very real.

As James wisely said, so I say to you as your brother:

Submit to God.

Resist the devil.

Make Satan flee.

Binding Demons

"...how can one enter into the house of the strong man, and plunder his goods, unless he first binds the strong man? Then he will plunder his house." The Lord Jesus Christ

Matthew 13:30 Let both grow together until the harvest, and in the harvest time I will tell the reapers, "First, gather up the darnel weeds, and bind them in bundles to burn them; but gather the wheat into my barn."'"

Matthew 14:3 For Herod having laid hold on John, did bind him, and did put him in prison, because of Herodias his brother Philip's wife,

Matthew 22:13 Then the king said to the servants,' Bind him hand and foot, take him away, and throw him into the outer darkness; there is where the weeping and grinding of teeth will be.'

Mark 3:27 But no one can enter into the house of the strong man to plunder, unless he first binds the strong man; and then he will plunder his house.

Mark 5:3 He lived in the tombs. Nobody could bind him any more, not even with chains,

Acts 9:14 Here he has authority from the chief priests to bind all who call on your name."

Acts 21:11 Coming to us, and taking Paul's belt, he bound his own feet and hands, and said, "Thus says the Holy Spirit:' So will the Jews at Jerusalem bind the man who owns this belt, and will deliver him into the hands of the Gentiles.'"

Revelation 20:2 ...and he laid hold on the dragon, the old serpent, who is Devil and Adversary, and did bind him a thousand years, and he threw him into the abyss, and shut it and sealed it over him, so that he would not deceive the nations any longer, until the thousand years were completed; after these things he must be released for a short time.

1210. Deo (deh'-o)
Bind, be in bonds, knit, lie, wind primary verb; to bind (in various applications, literally or figuratively) -- bind, be in bonds, knit, tie, wind. **Online Parallel Bible, Greek Lexicon**

I have heard some ministers say this about binding demons:

"If we can bind demons, then for how long is the demon bound?"

The tone in the question usually suggests that the one who asks it thinks he is clever, having shown once and for all the utter foolishness of thinking that a demon can be "bound," like a dog or donkey.

I quoted all the verses on the first page to show that the meaning of the word, in Greek or English, has to do with restraint of presence, speech, or action. So, the question above, put another way, is this, "if we can restrain a demons actions, for how long is he restrained?" Put this way, it doesn't seem like such a ridiculous notion, but an honest question that needs an honest answer. By the Spirit in me, for God's glory and the glory of the name of Jesus, I hope to give this answer.

First of all, we can indeed restrain demons. This is an issue of authority. We have been given authority over all of the power of the enemy, according to Jesus in the gospel of Luke chapter 10:19. "We" means those who believe in Him. And indeed, one of the signs of belief in Jesus is casting out demons. Again, this is an issue of authority. We can tell demons, as Jesus did, to be silent, inactive, and absent. We can stop them from talking, acting, or being present. We can "bind" them. We can keep them from accomplishing their goals, goals against Christ, His kingdom, and His gospel. We can, should, and must do this.

Here is where binding comes in. Jesus Himself used this analogy when He was accused of casting out demons by the authority of Beelzebub, the prince of demons. He made it clear that kingdoms and households cannot stand if they are divided. He showed that Satan, who seeks to inhabit and control men and women, would not go against himself in this matter. In this context Jesus speaks of "binding the strong man," an analogy for a demon taking over a house and all that is in the house. The body is compared to a house here and later when a demon leaves "his house" and comes back to "his house" and finds it swept and clean. The demon then goes to get seven more powerful than him.

As shown in the verses on the first page, Satan himself will be bound for 1000 years, literally bound, literally restrained, locked up, imprisoned. I will simply insert the name of the devil in the question about binding demons. "If Satan can be bound, then for how long is he bound?" In this situation, he is bound or imprisoned for 1000 years, then released. Please focus on the concept of imprisonment. I will use this to answer the question.

I, as I write, am a corrections officer, a detention deputy, an officer. I have the authority and power to bind and loose, to handcuff and unhand cuff; to open and close cell doors. I have keys by which I bind and loose.

Observe these verses:

"Behold, He tears down, and it cannot be rebuilt; He imprisons a man, and there can be no release. Job 12:14

"I will give you the keys of the kingdom of heaven; and whatever you bind on earth shall have been bound in heaven, and whatever you loose on earth shall have been loosed in heaven." Matthew 16:19

"To the angel of the church in Philadelphia write:

He who is holy, who is true, who has the key of David, who opens and no one will shut, and who shuts and no one opens, says this: 'I know your deeds. Behold, I have put before you an open door

that no one can shut, because you have a little power, and have kept
My *word, and have not denied My name." Revelations 3:7-8*

"Then I saw an angel coming down from heaven, holding the
key of the abyss and a great chain in his hand. And he laid hold of
the dragon, the serpent of old, who is the devil and Satan, and
bound him for a thousand years; and he threw him into the abyss,
and shut it and sealed it over him, so that he would not deceive the
nations any longer, until the thousand years were completed; after
these things he must be released for a short time.*

*When the thousand years are completed, Satan will be released
from his prison, and will come out to deceive the nations which are
in the four corners of the earth, Gog and Magog, to gather them
together for the war; the number of them is like the sand of the
seashore." Revelations 20:1-8*

Again, I am an officer, and I believe that the correlation is
exact, because according to Hebrews, the visible things that
exist were made from the invisible word of God. I believe
there is a spiritual correlation to all physical things.

The "clever question" concerning binding and loosing
implies this notion:

Why not just bind demons indefinitely or forever? If we
do not, then we have to keep binding them and loosing them
over and over again.

Well why not ask this question to God Himself?

Why allow Satan freedom to do anything at all, ever?
Why let him out of the pit at all, even for a "short time." Why
only 1000 years in his prison, verses forever? And why do we
have commands to resist the devil, put on the whole armor of
God, and be watchful? How long do we have to do these
things while on earth? "If we can resist the devil, how long
doe he remain 'resisted?'"

As an officer, for example, there are times in which the
inmates I guard are "locked down." They are "bound" for a
certain number of hours, and then loosed to eat, shower,
watch TV, etc. When an inmate goes to court, he is

handcuffed and shackled in chains, like the chain the angel used to bind Satan in his "prison."

THE TIME OF BINDING DEPENDS ON THE PURPOSE AND TERRITORY OF AUTHORITY.

I can't lock an inmate down indefinitely or handcuff him at will. The issue is purpose. For court dates, inmates are being transported from jail to court, and they are bound to prevent escape. They stand before the judge, bound, to prevent an attack upon the judge. When brought back to jail, they are loosed, because they are in "permanent" custody. The doors to the unit or dorm are locked. They cannot get out. They are banished from society. Yet in the facility binding and loosing happen constantly, depending the purpose and territory.

Before I take this back to the spiritual, I have another analogy.

I also used to be a bouncer at a bar. When a person was "disorderly" we could command them to leave and enforce this command by physically "kicking them out."

Command.

Eject.

We had to command them first. When this command was not obeyed, the person was at that point trespassing. Territory.

We could then "bind" the person with our hands and physically force them out of the bar. Once outside, they were on "city property" and under the authority/jurisdiction of the police. If the person refused to leave the area, we called the police. The police then commanded them to leave. If the person refused, he or she was trespassing after a warning, which is against the law, and taken into custody; bound in handcuffs and put in a police car, then taken to jail. How long were they bound? Until they got to jail. How long are they in jail? The judge determines this.

The bar didn't really care about where the person went or how long the person was in handcuffs, etc, AS LONG AS THEY LEFT THE BAR AND DIDN'T COME BACK UNTIL THEY WERE SOBER AND PAYING CUSTOMERS, SERVING THE PURPOSE OF THE BAR, WHICH WAS TO MAKE MONEY. This customer went against that purpose and could cause the bar to lose money as a liability. This customer could also cause the bar to lose its liquor license. So the bar just wants the person to leave for at least that night.

But there were three levels of "ineligibility" when it came to bar entry. In other words, there were three basic time frames that a person was "bound" from coming back to the bar:

1. Daily/nightly: this person was kicked out just for that day or night. But he/she could come back later/the next day, if they were sober and willing to pay and cooperate with the basic "bar rules," like no standing on the tables (which is a liability if the person has been drinking and he or she falls), etc.

2. Temporary: this applied to a person who had been recently fired or who quit. They were ineligible to enter for a month or so, but after that could return.

3. Permanently: these people had constantly caused so many problems that the bar could not allow them to ever return.

Now again, the clever questioner rightly assumes that there wouldn't be this kind of variation with demon presences. And there isn't in the same sense that the bar allows some people to return after being "cast out" of the bar. Of course we don't ever want demons around, and they never serve the purposes of God in our lives, at least directly or willingly, like customers may serve the purpose of the bar to make money. But these time frames do apply. Before I can show how, I have to show one more thing using bouncers as an analogy.

Bouncers were made aware of the eligibility statuses of customers or former employees. There was a list with names and dates of eligibility. Some were temporary, some were permanent. There was no list for daily/nightly ineligibility, but there was "pass on" information given between changing shifts. If I kicked someone out during the day shift, I would inform the night shift of the person, giving a description, so that the night shift person would watch for him or her and not allow him or her back in that day.

There are four possible responses to the three levels of ineligibility:

1.   Compliance: the bouncer enforces the eligibility statuses. If he sees someone who is ineligible, he will not under any circumstance allow the person in. He will watch to make sure the person doesn't sneak in.

2.   Ignorance: a bouncer may fail to check the list, and as result let someone in because he doesn't know the person is not supposed to be in the bar for whatever length of time.

3.   Negligence: a bouncer can be distracted, not watchful, due to trying to get phone numbers from women or other distractions, and thus allow ineligible people to enter.

4.   Defiance: the bouncer may not agree with a certain person being ineligible and allow them in any way, knowingly, willingly, and purposely.

PLEASE NOTE THESE TWO VERY IMPORTANT ASSUMPTIONS:

1.   IT WAS ASSUMED THAT MOST, IF NOT ALL, OF THE PEOPLE WHO WERE NOT SUPPOSED TO BE IN THE BAR KNEW THAT THEY WERE NOT SUPPOSED TO COME IN!! THEY KNEW!

2.   IT WAS ASSUMED THAT THEY WOULD TRY TO COME IN ANY WAY!!

This is crucial to our discussion. They know! They will
try to come in anyway! This is why you watch!! They
know!! They try! They sometimes succeed. They sometimes
fail. IT DEPENDS ON THE BOUNCER!! HE MUST
EXERCISE HIS AUTHORITY. HE MUST COMMAND. HE
MUST ENFORCE.

Albert knew he wasn't supposed to be in the bar. He
would actually tell the new people this. Yet he would still try
to come in. Every now and then I would see him standing at
a counter. I would look at him. He would smile and leave.

Demons know that they have no authority over believers.
They know this. They have permanent ineligibility. Yet they
try. Sometimes they succeed. Sometimes they fail. It
depends on the Christian. If the Christian is ignorant, he will
not even know that the demon is present in his life. If he is
negligent, he may know of the possibility, but fail to be
"watchful," as both Peter and Paul command us to be in
relation to our enemy. Keyword: enemy. If she is defiant,
meaning living in rebellion or sin, she is welcoming the devil,
the king of all rebels, and the demons, who love rebellion.
But if she is compliant, she will watch and stand against
Satan and demons, actively, consciously, knowing that the
enemy seeks OPPORTUNITY.

But, when you are dealing with others, for example,
nonbelievers, you are dealing with people who do not have
authority over demons or the power of the enemy. The
nonbeliever is defiant, negligent, and ignorant of Satan's
schemes. In this situation, if for example you go to a
nonbeliever's house for dinner, you have authority over all of
the power of the enemy, including the enemies' power over
this nonbeliever. The enemy seeks to blind the non-Christian
to the light of the gospel, to put in place obstacles to his
belief. You have the authority to bind demons in this
situation, or stop them from doing this WHILE YOU ARE
INTERACTING WITH THE NONBELIEVER. Of course you

can continue to pray for them and against the enemy in relation to them. But you cannot take direct authority over demons in relation to this non-Christian because the person has freewill, and if he doesn't yield to God, then he gives access to demons, knowingly or unknowingly. This is not as dramatic as "demon movies" make it seem, though possession is very real. But realize this: demons usually want to be undetected, because they are liars and deceivers, just like the person who is not supposed to be in the bar usually hides, or even changes clothes or puts on a hat, which is why we have to watch carefully. Usually people with fake identification who tried to get in the bar paid good money for a good fake id, so we had to watch to detect deception. Thus demons will not usually be obvious.

In summary of these points: believers have authority over demons, though they may be ignorant, negligent, or defiant in relation to their authority. Non believers do not have authority over demons, but are under the authority of demons, knowingly or unknowingly, willingly or unwillingly. The believers' authority over all the power of the enemy is constant in their own lives and circumstances, as long as they are not ignorant, negligent, or defiant. Their authority in other circumstances or in relation to other people is limited to the time they are in those circumstances and in relation to those people, because these people, whether nonbelievers or immature believers, must exercise their authority in their own circumstances.

A bouncer or police officer has jurisdiction, or a limited territory of authority. A customer cannot kick someone out of a bar, and a citizen cannot make an arrest. But the customer can go to the security guard, and a citizen can call the police. And the believer can cast a demon out of a nonbeliever if the nonbeliever wants, or bind demons in relation to the nonbeliever if the nonbeliever is open to truth and the authority of God.

So, we now get to the question at last: How long is a demon bound?

In situations where you have authority, you can bind them permanently. For example, in one situation when casting out a demon, Jesus told the demon to leave the child who was possessed and to NEVER RETURN. As a parent, I can do this with my children in the name of Jesus, knowing that I act in agreement with Jesus' authority, character, and power. Now remember, the demon will try to find a way back into the life he left; an opening; an opportunity; in a word: permission. The demon, though "permanently ineligible" to influence believers, will nevertheless still try to effect believers, just like people who were permanently ineligible to enter the bar, and knew they were ineligible, still tried to enter the bar. We are dealing with rebels here.

A Christian writer named Watchman Nee said wisely: "nothing pertaining to man can be accomplished without the consent of his will." This is positive and negative. No good thing can happen to us unless we agree, and no bad thing can happen to us unless we agree. This doesn't mean good or evil can't surprise us. It just means that our response to that good or evil, the acceptance or rejection of it, is up to us.

Therefore, in positions of authority, we can bind demons permanently, but we must remain watchful, and we must make sure those under our authority give no opportunity of permission of demonic entry.

Recall again, the one permanently banished from the bar knows it and yet tries to get back in. If I am at the door, then Albert won't try to come in. But if one of the negligent bouncers is at the door, this bouncer will allow Albert in the bar. He is still permanently ineligible, but his status is not being enforced. So it is with demons. A husband or father can permanently bind a demon in relation to his children and his wife. But his wife must be in agreement, never negligent, or defiant of the husbands command. If she is negligent or

defiant, then when the husband isn't around, she may allow a
demon's influence upon her or their children.

When you are in a place temporarily, you can bind
demons from the time you enter until the time you exit; from
the time you are present until you are absent you can take
authority over all the power of the enemy, as Christ said; for
the purpose of the work God has you to do at the time and
place of ministry. Note: you are not permitting demons to
return when you leave. Hopefully there will be those who
remain who agree with the binding of the enemy and will
continue to enforce it when you leave. But if there is not, the
best you can do is pray that the works of the devil be
destroyed and that the work that God did through you will
remain. Yet people must renounce the world and embrace
the kingdom of God. They must renounce lies and embrace
the truth. If this is not done, demons can and will return
wherever they are allowed to do so.

For example, if a preacher is invited to a church to speak,
this preacher can bind the demons for the purpose of the
message accomplishing its goal, whether conviction leading
to salvation of non-believers, or edification leading to further
ministry for believers. The demons are bound, rendered
silent, inactive, and absent, in the name of Jesus, by the power
of the Holy Spirit, for the glory of God the Father. The
preacher preaches. Those who have ears to hear, they hear.
Those whose hearts are receptive, like good soil, receive the
"seed" of God's word, and God's word "bears fruit" in their
lives. But there are those who refuse to listen to what God
says, and Satan, like a bird, comes and takes the seed (the
word) from their hearts, which Jesus compares to a ground of
stone that won't receive seeds. Satan is allowed to do this
with the hard headed person, but not with those who had
open their minds and hearts to hear God. So in this situation,
he was bound as long as there was receptivity to what God

says. The moment the person listens to and trusts God, he is no longer bound.

Another example is a babysitter. If a young Christian woman is hired by a non-Christian to baby sit, the Christian can bind demons from the time she begins baby sitting until she leaves. In other words, wherever a believer is, if that believer is in the Spirit, neither defiant nor negligent or ignorant, then Satan and Demons are bound as long as that believer is present AND ACTIVELY ENFORCING THE AUTHORITY OF THE KINGDOM OF GOD.

Demons are "bound" or restrained as long as you enforce your authority where you are at the moment. This is the answer to the question.

You have authority over all of the power of the enemy.

This doesn't mean he won't attack or tempt you. It just means that you can successfully resist the devil and take authority over him in union with Christ, and that when you do this, the devil will literally flee from you.

I hope you are encouraged and enlightened in the authority God gave you as a believer. In the name of Jesus, do what He did: Destroy the works of the devil. Whatever the devil does, undo. Oppose him wherever you are, actively and consciously. He is your enemy. Give glory to God in doing this. Amen.

The Fruit of the Spirit

INTRODUCTION

"Be fruitful and multiply."God, to Adam and Eve
"Abide in me and I in you, that you may bear much fruit."
    Jesus to the 12 Apostles
"You will know them by their fruit." Jesus to His disciples

God clearly desires fruitfulness. He desired it in the beginning and does so until the very end. He rewards the fruitful life at judgment, expressed in the parable of the talents and seen in His judgments of the seven churches of Asia in the book of Revelations.

Recently I came to believe that the only way to truly know a believer in Christ is by the fruit of the Spirit. Charles Stanley, one I respect as gifted by the Holy Spirit in teaching, said that it is the proof of the believer's life in the Spirit, not a proof, but the proof. I believe what he says is true. The fruit brings about unity among believers and attracts nonbelievers, as Stanley also said. Gifts are the manifestations of the Spirit's power, but I believe fruit are the manifestation of His character, and should therefore be the foundation and motivation of the spiritual gifts, as I believe Paul illustrates in I Corinthians Chapter 13 and 14. One should not focus on fruit, but on following the Spirit, which naturally results in fruit. The Spirit produces the fruit. The believer simply bears the fruit the Spirit produces. This connects with what Christ said about Him being the true vine and His disciples the branches. As the branch simply stays connected to the vine and thus bears fruit effortlessly, so we stay connected to Christ and we bear fruit effortlessly.

But how do we stay connected to Christ? How do we "walk in the Spirit?" Or how does being led by the Spirit, which seems synonymous with walking in the Spirit, practically happen?

I will focus on two ways I believe we abide in Christ, or live in agreement with the Spirit. I will also express what it means to follow the Spirit's lead, or to be led by the Spirit. I pray that God will enlighten me as I write, that I may experience what I say to you, and that you may experience what I say, as the Spirit gives me words for me and for you. I ask this of God in the name of Jesus Christ our Lord and Savior. Amen.

ABIDE

Christ is a person. He makes an analogy of abiding in Him as a branch does with a vine. This connection is one of being a member, organically. Indeed, we are branches and body parts. This union is so complete that separation means death to the branch or the body part, disconnection or dissection/amputation. But what does this mean in actual experience?

John gives the answers in his gospel and his first epistle.

It seems to me that abiding in Christ, or being intimately connected to Him, is summed up in total submission and total obedience.

Observe:
Christ said that if "His words abide in you," and "if you keep my commandments you will abide in my love."
There it is.
To abide in Him is to obey Him. For Him to abide in us is for us to have and keep his word, or His command. This is the prerequisite for friendship and intimate fellowship, for the very manifestation of the Father and Son in our lives.
Observe again:

"He who has My commandments and keeps them, it is he who loves Me. And he who loves Me will be loved My Father, and I will love him and manifest Myself to him."

"You are My friends if you do whatever I command you."

Our will is to be Christ's will, so much so that we experience organic connection, the spontaneous connection between vine and branch or head and body. There is no obstruction between the vine and the branch. The sap of the vine freely flows into to branch. I believe the sap is the Spirit filled and inspired word of God, direct communion with the Holy Spirit through His spoken and written word. And there is also no obstruction between the head and the body. The spinal cord connects the brain to the rest of the body. I believe the Spirit is like the spinal cord. We are to be so connected to Christ, our head, by the Spirit, that even the hint of His inclination leads us to instant word and action. We have "the mind of Christ." Paul was able to speak as one trustworthy when he had no command from the Lord. Why? Because he was so one with God, and knew Him so well, that he could speak for Him accurately.

So, in summary, John the apostle gives the practical means to the end of abiding in Christ:

-Now he who keeps His commandments abides in Him, and He in him. And by this we know that He abides in us, by the Spirit He has given us.

-Whoever confesses that Jesus Christ is the Son of God, God abides in him, and he in God.

My wife knows me. She knows what I like and dislike, what I tolerate and what I find intolerable. She knows me. Therefore, in certain situations, without asking me or consulting with me, she could speak for me or answer for me. So it should be between Christ, our Vine, and us, His branches; we His body and Christ our head. This is connecting. This is abiding. Submit ones self to Christ so entirely that one intends like He intends, thinks like he thinks, speaks like He speaks, and acts like He acts. When two are one, in agreement, this is not only possible and probable, but also real, not just an ideal.

WALK

"Can two walk together unless they are agreed?" Amos 3:3

The prophet's question assumes two things:
1. The "two walking together" are people
2. The answer to the question is no.

The Holy Spirit testifies with our spirit that we are children of God.
The Holy Spirit
Our spirit
Both spirits "testify" or bear witness. Only people or persons can testify. In this matter the Holy Spirit and our spirits agree. They "walk together" in this way.
So imagine two people going the same place at the same time for the same reason. How could this be? How do you imagine it to be?
For example,
A man and a woman go to a 7:00 movie, the same 7:00 movie; 7:00 P.M. They sit in the same row and also right next to each other, one in seat 26, and the other in seat 27. They talk and laugh and hold hands during the movie. What would an onlooker assume about these two? It would be assumed that they knew each other and that they talked to each other before coming to the movies.
Intimate knowledge
Intimate communication
I believe this is what it means to "walk in (agreement with) the Spirit" or to be led by the Spirit.

A follower decides to indeed go where the leader goes. He gives up the liberty of determining his own direction. She gives up her will for the will of the one who leads. In this way, two walk together who have agreed to do so.

This is what should be the case between the children of God and the Holy Spirit who is in them. But how do spirits commune with each other? I believe they commune the same way souls commune, by way of speech.

Don't angels and demons talk in the Bible, whether to each other or to humans? Angels and demons are persons, though spirits. They may not have physical vocal cords, but they do have the ability to speak, and indeed in human languages.

In the book of Acts I see the Spirit speaking. He is referred to as the one who spoke through the mouth of David and the prophets. He speaks to Peter and Phillip and through Agabus and the prophets and teachers at Antioch. Why would He, a Person in us, not speak to us, when He clearly has the ability to do so? Jesus said that He would not "speak" on His own, but would "speak" only what He hears, and would "tell us" what was yet to come. The Spirit will speak and tell, according to Jesus.

To follow the Spirit is to listen to Him and obey what He says. Because He is the Spirit of Christ, then what is true of Christ is true of Him. If you have and keep the Spirit's commands, you love the Spirit and you are friends with the Spirit. And I believe that the fruit of the Spirit is the result of this love and friendship between the Spirit of God and the spirit of the saint. The one who is truly following the Spirit manifests the fruit of the Spirit.

How do you follow Him, or listen to Him? How do you know the difference between The Spirit, Satan, or yourself?

Paul and John tell us specifically how to know when the Spirit of God is truly inspiring a person who claims to be speaking by the leading of the Holy Spirit.

In the context of spiritual gifts, specifically the gifts of tongues/interpretation and prophecy, which will be Paul's focus in his discussion, "No one can say that Jesus is Lord except by the Holy Spirit."

In the context of not believing every spirit, testing the spirits, and being cautious of the "many false prophets that had gone out into the world," John said, "By this you know THE SPIRIT OF GOD, EVERY spirit (of every prophet) that confesses that Jesus Christ has come in the flesh is of God, and every spirit (of every prophet) that does not confess that Jesus Christ has come in the flesh is not of God. (Note what Paul says to the Corinthians about the "spirits" of prophets being subject to prophets. Based upon this, I believe it is a good interpretation to assume that John means spirits of prophets as well as demonic spirits posing as angels.)

So, the one claiming to have a message from God, or to be a messenger of God, an oracle, a prophet, will give the "testimony of Jesus" which is "the spirit of prophecy."

But this one, though he indeed may be a prophet, though she indeed may have the gift of prophecy, may not be holy. In other words, God gives gifts and does not take away the effectiveness of them based upon the person's character. For example, Balaam could prophecy even though he was corrupt. Samson still had strength from the Holy Spirit. Saul was still anointed king of Israel. Judas still healed and cast out demons. The Corinthians themselves did not lack any spiritual gifts. But they did lack the fruit of the Spirit, which is love, manifest in joy, peace, patience, kindness, goodness, faithfulness, gentleness, and self-control, against such there is no law, and those who follow the Spirit are therefore not subject to the law, and need not be; because the law is for transgressors and thus reveals transgressions and selfish inclination.

Therefore, the second way you know whether you are really hearing from the Holy Spirit is by the result of what would happen in you if you do what the voice says. If you obey the leading, will the result be love, manifest in joy, peace, patience, kindness, goodness, faithfulness, gentleness, and self-control; the fruit of the Spirit? Or will there be adultery, fornication, uncleanness, lewdness; sorcery, hatred, an outburst of wrath, dissension, contention, murder, drunkenness, jealousy, heresy, envy, revelry, or things like this; the works of the flesh? The works of the flesh are obvious. If you are being led to say or do anything that results in a work of the flesh, then the leading is from the flesh, and not the Spirit.

So, is there the testimony of Jesus as Lord, having come in the flesh; and is love the motivation, expressed in edification?

If these two things are in place, then you know that the voice you hear is none other than the Holy Spirit.

A demon spirit will not willingly or freely acknowledge Jesus as Lord. It will not focus upon the crucifixion and resurrection, both, which expose the defeat and humiliation of Satan. Demons will not inspire agape love, or love that takes no credit for itself and gives all credit to God. Demons will not give joy that comes from within and is not based in sensual or soul satisfaction. There is no true peace from demons, which is peace with God and from God that surpasses human understanding. There is definitely no true patience, for the flesh must have what it wants now. There is no kindness or goodness because the flesh is selfish. There is no faithfulness, because the flesh is ruled by emotion or sensation, which is always in fluctuation. There is no gentleness, but harshness and rudeness because of selfishness. And there is definitely no self-control, but rather some object of self-gratification that the flesh cannot and will not deny, an object that controls the one in the flesh.

So, if you want to bear the fruit of the Spirit, these principles of abiding and walking should be remembered and applied:

Exchange your will for the will of the Spirit.

Seek to be a witness of the Lord Jesus, which is the reason the Spirit is in you.

Seek to edify believers and to convict nonbelievers and carnal believers by the Spirit.

If YOU do these three things, consciously, knowingly, willingly, and actively, YOU will know YOUR OWN THOUGHT OR INTENT. In other words, you know the Holy Spirit by the testimony of Christ and the fruit of the Spirit. You know Satan by the testimony of the Antichrist and the works of the flesh. (By the testimony of the antichrist I mean the opposite of every thing Jesus stands for. Christ is humble. The antichrist is prideful. Christ seeks only the glory of God the Father; the antichrist only seeks his own glory.) And you know you because you are the one who is choosing to apply the three principles given above.

Once you do the three things above, the next step is the practical experience of following the Spirit. I give three suggestions based upon three levels of communication between the Spirit and you:

Conscience

Intuition

Communion

Paul consistently made reference to his conscience. One specific reference is this:

"I have hope in God that there will be a resurrection of the dead, both of the just and the unjust. This being so, I myself always STRIVE TO HAVE A CONSCIENCE WITHOUT OFFENSE TOWARDS GOD AND MAN."

Note again words from Paul: "I tell the truth in Christ, I am not lying, my conscience also bearing me witness IN THE

HOLY SPIRIT, that I have great sorrow and continual grief in my heart."

So clearly Paul considered conscience a trustworthy guide. Some object to this, saying that scripture is the only trust worthy guide. But scripture itself disagrees with this. Note that Paul in First Corinthians chapters 8-10 deals with conscience verses so called "knowledge." Some of the "stronger" more "mature" and "knowledgeable" Corinthians felt free to eat food sacrificed to idols, "knowing" indeed this scripture, "The earth is the Lord's and the fullness thereof." Knowing therefore that all food comes from God and not idols, and that idols did not truly exist in themselves, and in themselves were nothing, they were free in this matter of eating. However, younger, "weaker" believers were convicted in their conscience about food sacrificed to idols. What did Paul say? He told the strong and knowledgeable not to cause the weak to stumble and sin by offending their weak consciences. He also affirmed their weak conscience by showing how the knowledgeable Israelites, all having first hand knowledge of the one true God and of his law, still worshipped idols. He warned the knowledgeable ones to beware when they think they stand lest they fall. Indeed, are the "weaker" believers to disregard conscience and apply the scripture known by the "stronger" believers? No. In fact, the stronger are to respect the conscience of the weak, even though they have scripture knowledge.

Now of course, the Holy Spirit filled conscience agrees with scripture. I am simply establishing the fact that scripture itself, through Paul, affirms the trustworthiness and value of conscience.

Having done this, I say to you that the first step to knowing the voice of the Holy Spirit is to be faithful to your conscience. Watchman Nee said:

"To be faithful to one's conscience is the first step towards sanctification."

Your conscience will keep you from the flesh, or convict you if you are in the flesh. But if you are faithful to your conscience, you will bear the fruit of the Spirit

Next is "intuition," which is a level above conscience. Though this word is not a specifically "scriptural" word, it communicates what we understand in today's language about the Spirit's leading. By intuition I simply mean direct revelation without outside cause or reason. You "just know" something, though you can't explain how you know it, your knowledge is accurate, and it is beneficial to edify believers or convict nonbelievers, leading them to Christ. Though it is not "clairvoyance" or "mind reading" or "psychic ability," I believe these are perversions or demonic versions of the truth. A believer will be able to "sense" in varying degrees the thoughts and intents of the hearts of others just as Jesus was able to. Those very strong in this ability have the "gift of discerning spirits." They are able to detect the spiritual origin of a situation or teaching, whether from God, man, or Satan.

If you are faithful to your conscience, meaning you consistently heed it and repent if needed, never seeking to silence or soften your conscience through justification or rationalization, then you will receive more specific revelation. Conscience in the beginning tends to simply focus on right and wrong. Then it focuses not just on right and wrong, but what is of God and what is not, even if dealing with two good or right objects. The more faithful a servant is, the more revelation and light God will give. You will not just have "checks" in your spirit, or the "red light/green light," or the "peace/lack of peace," or the "not 'feeling right' about something," but you will have specific supernatural insights, knowing things beyond your five senses or your reasoning. You will sense that you should talk to a specific person a specific time. You have a strong feeling about a person, or you "can't get a person off of your mind." So you call the person and he says, "It's so funny that you called. I have

been thinking about you all day and wanting to talk to you."
And the person crucially needed this very conversation. This
is an example of you following the Spirit. But there are times
when God's children don't follow, and then they realize a
missed opportunity and say things like, "'something' told me
to call that person." If you follow "intuition," you will follow
the Spirit and bear the fruit of the Spirit.

Finally there is communion. This means the Spirit
simply tells you what to do, in English words.

Some people speak of a "word" from God. They start
out hearing one word, or small phrases, or simple sentences.
The same is true, mind you, with those who speak in
tongues/interpret or prophecy. And why wouldn't it be?
Think of babies. Parents talk to babies from the time they exit
the womb, literally. But babies don't understand them at all.
The baby cries. Someone comes. Things are better. This is
the communication in the beginning.

Pleasure or displeasure (conscience)

Physically stopping the child or giving certain things
when the baby cries (intuition)

Simple commands and conversation (communion)

Advanced commands and conversation (communion)

Note: the parents verbally and literally talk to the child
from birth. The child's immaturity and small vocabulary
limit his or her understanding. With growth in maturity and
vocabulary, the child and parent can directly talk to each
other.

I believe it is exactly the same with the Holy Spirit and
us.

Therefore, if you do not feel you know God's voice, be
true to your conscience. I believe the process I described will
come naturally. Then you will be holy, bearing the fruit of
the Spirit as you use the gifts of the Spirit. Christ will be seen
in you in character (fruit) and power (gifts.)

I share one more thing, and then I am done.

Just as each believer has certain spiritual gifts, I believe each believer will manifest a certain "emphasis" of the fruit of the Spirit, which is love. For example, all are not evangelists, but all are witnesses. Though all do not have the spiritual gift of faith, all are to have faith. Though all do not have the gift of encouragement, all are to encourage. Though all are not apostles, all are "sent" to be witnesses.

In the same way, all of us are to bear the fruit of the Spirit, which is love, but I believe it will be manifest differently in different people, and that all of the aspects of the fruit of the Spirit are connected. For example, the one who loves may be supernaturally patient, which will result in joy in whatever circumstance, peace, self-control, etc. Or the one who is bearing the fruit of joy will be loving and peaceful as well, being kind, good, gentle, and faithful, and because of contentment, he or she will be in control of himself/herself. Some may "naturally" rejoice in the Lord always. Some may have a supernatural calm no matter what is going on around them. I don't mean that a person is simply a "laid back person," or a "positive person." I mean a character trait that cannot be explained other than by the resurrection of Christ. In other words, since the word for "fruit" is singular, I don't believe we have to try to bear all nine of the fruit, but that all of the fruit are connected, and that each believer may have an emphasis in one of the manifestations of love that connect all the rest.

Do you see what I mean? Each believer has a specific emphasis of the Spirit's power (gifts) and character (fruit.) I don't believe bearing the fruit of the Spirit is to be difficult, any more difficult than it is for a branch to bear the fruit of the vine. The branch does this naturally and effortlessly. And in the same way, I believe we will all use our spiritual gifts and bear spiritual fruit without effort and strain. So look for the manifestation of love in your life as you follow the Spirit that comes most effortlessly and is supernatural, that which is not something you were from birth, but from the time you were born again. And look for a burden or passion of action that you also did not have from birth, but from your rebirth. Here you will find the fruit and the gifts of the Spirit in your life, and you will be a blessing to everyone you encounter, bringing glory to God the Father and Son!

Be blessed with the experience of these words. Amen.

81

Power

"You will receive power when the Holy Spirit has come upon you." Acts 1:8a

Dunamis: ability, power, strength
Force (literally or figuratively); especially, miraculous power (usually by implication, a miracle itself) **Online Parallel Bible**

"And you shall be My witnesses both in Jerusalem, and in all Judea and Samaria, and even to the remotest part of the earth." Acts 1:8

Power.
Witnesses.

I see both of these in the book of Acts.

On the day of Pentecost, a mighty rushing wind and flaming tongues was experienced tangibly, literally. The disciples were filled with the Holy Spirit and spoke with other tongues as the Spirit gave them utterance. Others heard the miracle. Peter spoke concerning the miracle, by the miracle. He bore witness to the resurrection of the Lord Jesus Christ. 3,000 were saved.

A man lame from birth received the ability to walk by the name of Jesus, by the power of the Holy Spirit in Peter. This power bore witness to the name of the resurrected and ascended Savior. Peter again bore witness with the power of the Holy Spirit who filled him.

Angels unlocked prison doors.

The word could not be stopped, and miracles, signs, wonders, healings, and casting out of demons continued. Power, reverence, and unity characterized the early church.

Phillip and Stephen, servants of Christ in the body, performed great miracles, signs, and wonders. Stephen's words could not be resisted or refuted. Both bore witness with power and by power to the resurrection.

Peter and Cornelius received visions from heaven and met based upon them. The Holy Spirit fell upon Cornelius and his family, and they spoke in tongues and prophesied. The Spirit fell upon them, Gentiles, just as He fell upon the Jews in the beginning, on the day of Pentecost.

Power.
Witness.

Continually I see testimony in the book of Acts, confirmed by power.

Jesus appears to Saul on the road to Damascus. By brother Annanias, Paul received his sight and the filling of the Holy Spirit. Immediately Paul bore witness to the Christ as the Son of God.

Paul and Barnabas went on their first mission in agreement with a prophetic word from Agabus, a prophet.

They went on their second mission by the word of the Holy Spirit through prophets and teachers.

The Spirit forbid them to enter one place and did not permit them to enter another, but gave a vision about Macedonia. Paul and Barnabas knew by the vision that they should go there.

Power.
Witness.

Paul did "unusual miracles," assuming usual miracles existed.

Paul cast out demons and healed, and the Greeks sought to worship him as Hermes, and Barnabas as Zeus.

Phillip's power impressed a powerful magician, who came to the Lord. Peter's power also impressed this magician, who received a rebuke from Peter for wanting to buy the power of the Holy Spirit that Peter clearly had, power to impart the Holy Spirit to others; an impartation that the magician (named Simon) could clearly see. Phillip heard the voice of an angel and of the Holy Spirit Himself, as did Peter in relation to Cornelius. Phillip miraculously left the presence of the Ethiopian Eunuch.

Power.
Witness.

Paul received knowledge concerning shipwreck and a deadly serpent by no means harmed him. On the island of his banishment he healed the sick, bearing witness to the Name.

Having briefly surveyed Acts, it is clear that the church is to be a powerful witness of the resurrection of Jesus, a miraculously powerful witness.

This power should at least be miraculous boldness and effectiveness in utterance, meaning believers should possess power in their words that convince the hearers that Jesus is Lord and that He rose from the dead. This should be power to convict people of sin. It should also be power to reveal the secrets of the heart (prophecy, as Paul said in First Corinthians chapter 14.) It should be praise that reveals the presence of the One praised. It should be a proclamation with demonstration, proclaiming the coming kingdom, and demonstrating the nature and power of the kingdom to come.

How does a believer in the Lord Jesus receive this power in actual, practical experience?

I will tell you how I received power from God. I do not say that your experience must be same as mine, but also do not say that it cannot be the same. God does not show favoritism, but we are all different. If you want to receive power the way I did, I believe you can, and thus I share what God did for me.

I heard the word of God concerning evidence of being empowered by the Holy Spirit, or of being filled with the Spirit.

I believed what I heard.

I acted upon what I heard.

Hear.

Believe.

Act.

This is what I heard:

One of the signs that Jesus said would follow those who believe in Him is that they would speak a new, supernatural, spiritual language; a language unlearned by imitation, association, duplication; in other words, a language not learned by the natural process by which languages are usually learned, but one received immediately and spontaneously. This new language is called "tongues."

On the day of Pentecost, every disciple was filled with the Holy Spirit and spoke with other languages (tongues) as the Spirit gave them the ability (utterance)

When a soldier named Cornelius and his family were filled with the Spirit, they spoke with other tongues (unknown supernatural language directed to God) and prophesied (known supernatural speech directed to people from God)

When the Ephesians believers were filled with the Holy Spirit by the laying on of hands by Paul, they spoke with other tongues.

Jesus promised this as one of the signs that would follow those who believe.

In Luke 11:13-14, He said that as earthly fathers, even evil ones, knew how to give good gifts to their children, the very good things that their children ask for, so the heavenly Father gives the Holy Spirit to those who ask. If a child asks for bread, an earthly father, even an evil one, does not give a rock. If a child asked for a fish, he doesn't receive a serpent. If he asks for an egg, he doesn't get a scorpion. Note: Satan tempted Jesus to turn rocks into bread. Note also that snakes and scorpions are associated with the power of the enemy. Therefore, I believe it a safe interpretation that if a believer sincerely asks for the Holy Spirit, denying him/herself, and wanting to be filled with the Spirit and empowered by the Spirit, to be a witness of the resurrection, God will not give him Satan or a demon.

Though tongues are not the only sign of being filled with the Spirit, they are a legitimate one. Paul gave a command in his letter to the Corinthians not to forbid speaking in tongues. Anyone who forbids speaking in tongues disobeys God's command through Paul. Paul does not give a conditional command or a time-based command, meaning "do not forbid speaking in tongues until 'that which is perfect comes.'" He could have said this plainly. It is not enough to assume that he implied this. And if tongues would simply cease at a certain time, then he need not command it to not be forbidden, for how can it be forbidden after it ceases? Some may say, "Well, until tongues ceased, they were not to be forbidden." But why didn't he say this? Why didn't he make it clear that if tongues are spoken after they have ceased, i.e., after the canon of scripture is penned, then the tongues spoken are from demons? This is serious and not just a "minor theological issue" that we can "agree to disagree" upon. If tongues have ceased, all who claim to speak with new tongues are either demon possessed or suffering some psychological episode. But if they have not ceased, then be careful that you do not blaspheme the Holy Spirit, calling an act of the Holy Spirit an act of demons or of possible insanity.

So, having said this, here is how you can receive the filling of the Holy Spirit:

1. Ask for it according to the promises and commands given in scripture. Ask God to fill you with His Spirit and for it to be made evident by giving you the ability to speak by supernatural power as a witness of the resurrection.

Mark 16:17 and Acts 1:8 give promises that can be claimed

Roman 8:14 gives a principle

Ephesians 5:18 gives a command

I John 5:14-15 gives the assurance that when we ask anything in agreement with God's will, we know He hears us and grants our petition.

The verses I have just given assure you that it is God's will for you to be filled with the Holy Spirit so that you may be a witness of the resurrection of the Lord Jesus where ever you are, for "the remotest parts of the earth" or "the end of the earth" includes where you are now and wherever you go on earth.

2. Then thank God as an expression of faith, that you take His words and promises to be true, that you trust Him to fulfill His promises. Scripture says that God cannot lie, and that when He speaks, He acts; and that when He promises He fulfills. So to thank Him is to acknowledge these things.

3. Take a breath, open your mouth and speak spontaneously. Note, I cannot teach you how to speak by the power of the Holy Spirit. A human cannot teach this by definition. It is a spiritual gift and not a natural one. It is a gift given to you. You are the one who will speak, and the Spirit will give you power to do so. It is not the Spirit speaking for you or through you without your active cooperation or against your will. THIS IS VERY IMPORTANT. IT IS THE DIFFERENCE BETWEEN THE SPIRIT LEADING AND A DEMON POSSESSING. SATAN OR A DEMON WANT YOUR MIND AND WILL TO BE PASSIVE. GOD THE HOLY SPIRIT WANT YOUR MIND AND WILL TO BE ACTIVE. Again, it is you speaking and

the Spirit giving you power to do so for the purpose of
bearing witness to the resurrection and ascension of Christ
Jesus the Lord.

Therefore, I suggest that if you are not certain that you
have the ability to speak with a new language, to simply and
genuinely praise God, thank God, or worship God in your
own natural way. Do this freely and continue to do this.
You do not need to be "emotional" or "weird." You don't
need to try to be anything other than what you are. If you
genuinely have emotion, by all means express it in praise.
But don't manufacture it. Surely a believer can thank and
praise God, even a young believer, if for nothing else than for
being saved and for sins being forgiven! Speaking as the
Spirit empowers you is as natural as speaking your native
language, but the origin is supernatural. Having asked to be
filled with the Spirit, having thanked God in faith, and
praising/thanking God, by faith, in sincerity, I assure you
that you will experience power from within you as you
speak. This may be a new language; a power in praising and
thanking Him that you know is not from you, that is
supernatural. You may also speak a message directly from
God, which is called prophecy. And you may also experience
the desire to proclaim the good news about the resurrection
of Jesus, having a boldness and confidence and effectiveness
that you cannot explain naturally. Note, this last expression
is the primary reason you have been filled with the Spirit, and
whatever the Spirit chooses to enable you to do, whether
tongues, prophecy, praise, or proclamation, ALL OF IT WILL
BE TO GLORIFY JESUS AS RESURRECTED LORD. IF THIS
IS NOT YOUR MOTIVE, YOU DO NOT AGREE WITH GOD,
HIS SON, OR HIS SPIRIT. I cannot tell you what the Spirit
will have you do to show you that you are filled, but I can tell
you that you will know it just as they knew it in the book of
Acts, because He is the same Spirit, the Spirit of Jesus, who is
the same yesterday, today, and forever.

Having been filled with the Holy Spirit, and having spoken as He gave you the ability, I encourage you to seek by faith your spiritual gift. This gift is your ministry, and this ministry is your activity, according to Paul in I Corinthians Chapter 12:1-4.

This gifts, ministries, and activities, given by the Spirit, are the manifestations of the Holy Spirit in the body of Christ. It is the Spirit tangibly experienced! Think of that!

Your gift is your job description in the body of Christ. It is indeed your ministry! It is indeed your activity, what you are supposed to be doing. Find a body of believers that will allow you and encourage you to use your gift.

Your motivation should be conviction or edification, conviction for non-believers or carnal believers, and edification for spiritual believers.

Freely you have been given, as Jesus said. Freely give.

In other words, once you have been filled with the Spirit, and once you know what your gift is, use it every opportunity you get in every situation and relation and vocation, as the Spirit leads you.

This is how you can know what gift the Holy Spirit gave you: A revelation of a burden.

This is what I mean.

Whatever God gave you to do is a passion in the heart of God that is also in yours. What do you want to see happen among the people of God that cannot happen without the supernatural power of God? Does your heart break because of sicknesses and disease? Perhaps you are a healer. Do you desire intimate direct connection to God, to know the mysteries and intimacies of God's heart?

Perhaps tongues and interpretation is your mission. Do you know with certainty God's will in specific situations? Perhaps you have the gift of faith. Do you want to give practical solutions to problems, and are you capable of this after hearing a problem; solutions that will further the kingdom of God? Perhaps you have the gift of wisdom. Do you perceive demons in situations or relations? Perhaps you have the gift of discernment?

Burdens, a passion, an irritation that won't go away, all give clues to your gift.

Supernatural success in dealing with these, joy in doing so, and affirmation from those whose needs are met supernaturally also affirm your gift. Love motivates you as it motivates God, who is love.

Therefore, what you love in the body, what motivates you in terms of strengthening believers or leading believers to the Lord is your ministry, and thus your gift.

Yet even if you are not yet sure of your spiritual gift, be filled with the Spirit and speak by the power of the Holy Spirit. The Spirit who fills you and leads you will surely lead you to your gift as well. I cannot emphasize enough that through out scripture, Old Testament and New Testament, when people were filled with the Spirit the usual immediate result was supernatural speech. In other words, the Spirit filled them, and then they spoke. In the Old Testament, they primarily prophesied. In the New Testament there was praise, proclamation, tongues, and prophecy. At times men of God received power for battle after being filled with the Spirit like Samson, Gideon, and David. But this was not usual. Words tended to follow the filling. When the elders in Israel received the Spirit under the ministry of Moses, they prophesied, even one who was in his tent and not among them, and Moses said he wanted all of Israel to have the Spirit. Saul prophesied in the company of prophets when the Spirit came upon him. Zechariahs prophesied about John the Baptist. Elizabeth, filled with the Spirit, spoke concerning Jesus. That is usually what you find: a statement like "John, filled with the Spirit, said."

So, wherever you are, be filled with the Spirit in that context.

If you are a husband, be filled with the Spirit and receive power to be a witness of the sacrificial love of Christ who died for His bride, the church.

If you are a wife, be filled with the Spirit and submit to your husband as the Spirit in the Church submits to Christ and seeks His glory.

If you are a father, be filled with the Spirit of God the Father and receive power to be a father like He is.

If you are a mother, be filled with the Spirit, and receive power to represent your husband, the father of your children, as Christ represents His Father.

If you are a child, be filled with the Spirit of God the Son, and be empowered to submit to your father as Christ submits to The Father.

If you are a governor, an employer or leader or administrator, be filled with the Lord, who is the Spirit, and be empowered to have all authority in heaven and on earth as the Son has all authority in heaven and on earth.

If you are an employee, be filled with the Spirit, and be empowered to submit to the one above you as Christ submits to the Father above him.

Be empowered by the Spirit to be who you are and to do what you are presently responsible to do. Paul said that all are to remain in the place they were when they were called to be a Christian, unless a way is made out of that place in God's will. So, wherever you are, be there in the presence and power of the Holy Spirit. You have received power. Do not have a "tarrying meeting." Do not wait, because the time of fulfillment is now. You have the Spirit if you believe in Jesus, and if you have asked to be filled, then you are indeed filled. You are now, at this moment, a miraculously powerful witness of the resurrection of the Lord Jesus Christ.

Now, know that each gift is a manifestation of the Holy
Spirit, who glorifies Christ. In other words, each gift or office
some how reveals Christ, just as each job or vocation or
function does, as already mentioned.

If you are an apostle, you are sent as Christ was sent. As
the Father sent Christ, Christ sends you. As Christ was
anointed by the Holy Spirit, so are you. YOU HAVE THE
SAME HOLY SPIRIT THAT JESUS HAD! YOU HAVE THE
SAME POWER THAT JESUS HAD!

If you are a prophet or prophetess, you are the word
made flesh as Christ was and is and ever will be. You speak
only what you hear as the Spirit does. You say only what the
Father tells you just as Jesus did. Jesus considered Himself a
prophet, and others considered Him a prophet. As was Jesus,
so are you by the Spirit who gives you utterance.

As He is, so are you. The testimony of Jesus is the spirit
of prophecy. The true prophet declares: Jesus is Lord. Jesus
Christ has come in the flesh. He or she edifies, exhorts,
comforts, convicts. He reveals mysteries in the present and
what is to come in the future, according to the grace God
gives him, and the measure of faith received.

If you are an evangelist, you proclaim the good news of
the kingdom as Christ did. You tell of the King who has
come, as Christ, the king, proclaimed His kingdom.

If you are a pastor, you are a shepherd, just as Christ was
and is and ever will be the Good Shepherd.

If you are a teacher, you are like Christ, the Rabbi.

If you speak with a new tongue or interpret tongues, you
pray in the name of Jesus, as He so effectively prayed. He
often withdrew to lonely or deserted places early in the
morning or through out the day, to pray. He prayed so
effectively that His disciples asked Him to teach them to
pray.

If you prophecy, you do so as He did, speaking words
from God to men.

If you give words of wisdom, you do so as He did, making known that He was greater than Solomon, whose wisdom took the breath from the Queen of Sheba.

If you give words of knowledge, you know facts supernaturally, just as Christ had supernatural knowledge of things or events in his day.

If you discern spirits, you do so a Christ did, who cast out demons, identifying them and silencing them. You know men's hidden thoughts and intentions, as did Christ.

If you do miracles, you do so as Christ did when He fed 5000 people, multiplying fish and bread.

If you do signs and wonders, you do as Christ did when He walked on water and was transfigured in glory.

If you heal, you do as He did, healing all who are oppressed of the devil.

If you have faith, as He did, so do you, when He cursed the fig tree.

If you are an administrator, you administrate as He did when He sent out the apostles in order, giving specific instructions.

If you encourage, you do as He did, when He said, "Peace be with you." and "Do not be afraid."

If you exhort, you do as He did, when He urged all to repent and follow Him.

And whatever your gift may be, you are as He was, and is, and will ever be.

You are one with Christ, and He is with you. You have His power and character, the fruit of the Spirit, which is love, and the gifts of the Spirit, the Holy Spirit Himself.

I encourage you to believe and act upon this belief.

The Lord is with you.

The Lord is in you.

The Lord surrounds you. He fills you.

He leads you.

He empowers you. Live in power. Amen.

93

Christian Emotion

"God saw all that He had made, and behold, it was very good. And there was evening and there was morning, the sixth day." Genesis 1:31

Then the LORD saw that the wickedness of man was great on the earth, and that every intent of the thoughts of his heart was only evil continually. The LORD was sorry that He had made man on the earth, and He was grieved in His heart. The LORD said, "I will blot out man whom I have created from the face of the land, from man to animals to creeping things and to birds of the sky; for I am sorry that I have made them." Genesis 6:5-7

Moses said to the LORD, "Please, Lord, I have never been eloquent, neither recently nor in time past, nor since You have spoken to Your servant; for I am slow of speech and slow of tongue." The LORD said to him, "Who has made man's mouth? Or who makes him mute or deaf, or seeing or blind? Is it not I, the LORD? "Now then go, and I, even I, will be with your mouth, and teach you what you are to say." But he said, "Please, Lord, now send the message by whomever You will." Then the anger of the LORD burned against Moses...Exodus 4:10-14

The LORD descended in the cloud and stood there with him as he called upon the name of the LORD. Then the LORD passed by in front of him and proclaimed, "The LORD, the LORD God, compassionate and gracious, slow to anger, and abounding in loving-kindness and truth; who keeps loving-kindness for thousands, who forgives iniquity, transgression and sin; yet He will by no means leave the guilty unpunished, visiting the iniquity of fathers on the children and on the grandchildren to the third and fourth generations." Exodus 34:5-7

He entered again into a synagogue; and a man was there whose hand was withered. They were watching Him to see if He would heal him on the Sabbath, so that they might accuse Him. He said to the man with the withered hand, "Get up and come forward!" And He said to them, "Is it lawful to do good or to do harm on the

Sabbath, to save a life or to kill?" But they kept silent. After looking around at them with anger, grieved at their hardness of heart, He said to the man, "Stretch out your hand." And he stretched it out, and his hand was restored. The Pharisees went out and immediately began conspiring with the Herodians against Him, as to how they might destroy Him. Mark 3:1-6

Now Jesus had not yet come into the village, but was still in the place where Martha met Him. Then the Jews who were with her in the house, and consoling her, when they saw that Mary got up quickly and went out, they followed her, supposing that she was going to the tomb to weep there. Therefore, when Mary came where Jesus was, she saw Him, and fell at His feet, saying to Him, "Lord, if You had been here, my brother would not have died." When Jesus therefore saw her weeping, and the Jews who came with her also weeping, He was deeply moved in spirit and was troubled, and said, "Where have you laid him?" They said to Him, "Lord, come and see." Jesus wept. So the Jews were saying, "See how He loved him!" But some of them said, "Could not this man, who opened the eyes of the blind man, have kept this man also from dying?" John 11:30-37

Jesus came with them to a place called Gethsemane, and said to the disciples, "Sit here while I go and pray over there." And He took with Him Peter and the two sons of Zebedee, and He began to be sorrowful and deeply distressed. Then He said to them, "My soul is exceedingly sorrowful, even to death. Stay here and watch with Me." Matthew 26:36-38

But they rebelled and grieved His Holy Spirit; Therefore He turned Himself to become their enemy, He fought against them. Isaiah 63:10

Do not grieve the Holy Spirit of God, by whom you were sealed for the day of redemption. Ephesians 4:30

Be quick to hear, slow to speak and slow to anger; for the anger of man does not achieve the righteousness of God. James 1:19-20

BE ANGRY, AND yet DO NOT SIN; do not let the sun go down on your anger, and do not give the devil an opportunity. Ephesians 4:26-27

"If your brother sins go and show him his fault in private; if he listens to you, you have won your brother. "But if he does not listen to you, take one or two more with you, so that BY THE MOUTH OF TWO OR THREE WITNESSES EVERY FACT MAY BE CONFIRMED. "If he refuses to listen to them, tell it to the church; and if he refuses to listen even to the church, let him be to you as a Gentile and a tax collector. "Truly I say to you, whatever you bind on earth shall have been bound in heaven; and whatever you loose on earth shall have been loosed in heaven. Matthew 18:15-18

Is anyone among you suffering? Let him pray. Is anyone cheerful? Let him sing psalms. Is anyone among you sick? Let him call for the elders of the church, and let them pray over him, anointing him with oil in the name of the Lord. James 5:13-14

INTRODUCTION

I used to totally hate and distrust emotions, viewing them as a fluctuating nuisance in the life of humanity. They seemed a hopeless source of stress, unable to be expressed or suppressed. If only I could be angry freely without sinning or raging or losing control. If only I could be angry in the right way for the right reason. If only I wasn't so quick to lose my temper, so insecure, so "sensitive." When can I cry and not be "weak?" Should I ever hold back tears?

Scripture gives validation and hope for emotions. God the Father, God the Son, and God the Holy Spirit all have and express their emotions.

Perfect emotions
Perfect expression of emotions

I quoted the scriptures earlier, taking a page and a half to do so, to establish the fact that Christians, those who aim to be "Christ like," can and should have emotions, and that the scriptures tells us how to do so. My hope is that the Holy

Spirit in me and in you, the believing reader, may be set free to feel and express emotions without sin. I need the Spirit's help in this, and I write to myself as well as to you.

Holy Spirit, our Helper, please help me the one who writes, and help also the one who now reads these word, to feel as You feel and to express our feelings as You express Your feelings. In the name of Jesus I ask this for the glory of God the Father, whom we are to reflect as Christ does. Amen.

THE NATURE OF EMOTIONS

The fear of the LORD is to hate evil; Pride and arrogance and the evil way and the perverted mouth, I hate." Proverbs 8:13

Let love be without hypocrisy. Abhor what is evil. Cling to what is good. Romans 12:9

....

All emotions, every emotion, can be summed up in two words:

Pleasure

Displeasure.

Whatever the feeling, it is a variation on the theme of pleasure or displeasure.

And every emotion has an object. If it does not, it is unnatural. This is crucial.

Something or someone or some situation pleases you.

Something or someone or some situation displeases you.

When there is nothing or no one or no situation, and you feel angry, this is usually attributed to some kind of "hormonal imbalance." In other words, something in the body is wrong. Or, some attribute this objectless emotion to a problem with the mind. A person's perception of a person or situation is inaccurate. Thus their emotions are inaccurate. This brings up a very important truth.

Emotions can be righteous or unrighteous.

Right

Or not right.

Correct or incorrect.

Right or wrong.

Usually women, in general, in American society, as far as I can see, are taught that every emotion is valid and should be expressed, no matter the consequences of the expression. Some women are taught that they have a right to feel everything they feel and that no one should contradict their emotions. Their emotions are untouchable, a standard in and of themselves. If they feel it, it's true and right and good. Suppression is the ultimate transgression and sin when it comes to some women and their emotions. Venting is encouraged, meaning having someone to pour all of their emotions on, no matter how negative, hurtful, or damaging the emotions may be to the one listening.

In general, men in America, as far as I can see, do not have the same latitude with their emotions. Women are usually allowed to hit, slap, yell at, and insult men, even openly, and men are supposed to "take it." The very same behavior from a man is viewed as "psychologically and physically abusive," and it should be viewed like this, because it is. But it is also abusive for a woman to do this to a man.

Even the supposed desire for a "sensitive man" can be misleading. This usually does not mean a man that is as sensitive or "emotional" as a woman, but rather a man that is sensitive to his woman's emotions.

But from the word of God we see that both men and women are to control their emotions, neither venting nor giving expression without discretion, nor suppressing them hypocritically, acting happy when they are not. God Himself is our example. But before we look at His example, let's review what has been said before, applying the two verses that began this segment.

1. Emotions are summed up in either pleasure or displeasure.
2. Emotions have an object.
3. Emotions can be right or wrong.

Scripture gives us the standard by which to judge our emotions. This is the standard:

Love good. Hate evil.

Or, put another way, be pleased when good is the object. Be displeased when evil is the object.

Therefore,

-If you and I are pleased with evil, our pleasure or emotion is wrong.

-If you and I are pleased with good, our pleasure or emotion is right.

Proverbs 8:13 and Romans 12:9 both speak of this. Observe another verse that communicates the same truth:

"(Love) does not rejoice in iniquity, but rejoices in the truth." I Corinthians 13:6

Note, love rejoices in the truth, assuming that iniquity is not truth. Here is another very important principle concerning right and wrong emotion:

One's perception, which leads to one's emotion, MUST BE ACCURATE OR FACTUAL IN ORDER TO BE RIGHT!

For example, a "girlfriend" sees her "boyfriend" hugging a beautiful woman affectionately. In a fit of rage, she runs over and slaps the man and the woman. They both look at her with shock. The slapped woman says, "Why did you slap me AND MY BROTHER?" Evidently, the girlfriend DIDN'T KNOW that her boyfriend had a sister, or didn't know who his sister was. Now what if she protests, "Well, I felt like you were being unfaithful to me?" Would her feelings be right in and of themselves? Of course not. They are wrong because she is misinformed. So, just because the girlfriend "felt" she had been wronged does not mean she actually had been. Though this situation is obvious, others are not as obvious. If

I "feel" like my wife is disrespecting me, it does not necessarily mean that she is. I must investigate my emotions and the specific reason for my emotions in order to know whether my feelings are right or wrong. But I must have the knowledge that my feelings can indeed be wrong. If I start from the premise that all emotions are by definition right, I am open to deception.

There is a difference between an emotion being right and being valid or valuable. In other words, in the example with the misinformed girlfriend, her hurt was valid and valuable and should be taken seriously. But she shouldn't have slapped the man and woman. If she approached the man and said, "I am really hurt that you would 'cheat' on me," he could say, "Sweetie, I love you and am not 'cheating' on you. The woman you saw me hugging is my sister. Please know that I am committed to you." This man would be honoring the emotion and yet showing it to be inaccurate. Most likely the emotion will change. If it does not, and if the woman becomes angrier, even in the face of evidence that shows the man to be telling the truth, then her emotions are even more wrong and clearly something is wrong with her.

Getting back to the verse in I Corinthians (about love rejoicing in truth,) to rejoice is an expression of emotion, of pleasure. Love takes no pleasure in iniquity but does take pleasure in truth. Therefore, this shows the standard of emotions, of humor and arousal and affection.

We do not control our emotions directly. We control them by the direct control of our mindset or attention or perception. In other words, we focus our minds on what we choose, and we can define what we focus upon according to the word of God, seeing it as God sees it, loving what He loves and hating what He hates. He is our example. Let us therefore look to Him to show us how we should feel.

GOD'S EMOTIONS

God was clearly pleased with all of His creation before the fall. In fact, after acts of creation, He looked upon what He made and declared it good. Why else would God do anything, being subject to no one, accountable to no one? And what else would be the standard of good and evil other than the perfect pleasure and displeasure of God, who is perfect and infinite and eternally good? Pleasure is by definition good, and displeasure not good. All that is good and perfect comes from God. All Satan can do is pervert pleasure, but he cannot create it. Indeed, Eden was a garden of delights, and heaven will possess no more pain or tears or sorrow. How could it? God is good, and heaven is His throne. "In His presence there is fullness of joy; at His right hand there are pleasures forever more."

Adam and Eve sinned, and after this had many children.

Later Noah was born, and he married and had three sons. In all the earth, Noah and his family alone were righteous. God saw and acknowledged this, and He saw and acknowledged the state of all mankind. Noah and his family alone found favor with God. All others God saw as unrighteous.

Being who He is, witnessing every imagination and intention of men being only evil all the time, what did God feel?
Grief
Regret
Sorrow.
God, the perfect, regretted ever making man. He not only felt this, rightly and perfectly, but He expressed it,

rightly and perfectly. Here we find the first lesson concerning emotion.

We should know exactly what we feel, why we feel it, and whether the feeling is based upon accurate perception, after thorough investigation. And we should not go beyond this knowledge of truth in expressing our emotions. Until we know that these things are so, we should remain silent and still, saying nothing and doing nothing. Otherwise our emotion and the expression of the emotion may be wrong.

God, having expressed what He felt and why He felt it to Noah, gives Noah instructions in relation to His emotions.

Here again, in Noah's situation, we learn from God.

Emotion is the fuel of action, motivation. In other words, once we know what we feel and why we feel it, we should seek the right way to express it in speech or action. If we encounter evil, for example, we should know what the evil is and why it is evil. We should find out the intention of the one doing evil, as we will discuss later. If we are in a position to remove the evil and replace it with good, we are obligated to do so. If we are not, we should seek one who is. If we can find no human who can remove the evil, we should seek God to do so.

This is what we find with God. He planned to destroy the earth and start over, if you will. But note: it took Noah 120 years to complete the ark, which of course God knew it would. Thus God gave evil humanity 120 years to repent. He is indeed true to His declaration of Himself to Moses:

Gracious and merciful
Slow to anger

Even with Moses, even in calling Moses, and with Moses' hesitation, God, who burned in anger towards Moses, did not judge him immediately or even seem to express His anger, as far as I can see in this scripture. But how "slow" is "slow," or how long should we wait before we express our anger? How do we find out what we are angry about and why we are angry about it? How do we not go too far in dealing with our anger? All of this is to come. But we must first see this in action with God Himself.

Jesus was angry with the hardhearted Pharisees, grieved by their stubbornness. Why? These would rather help an animal on the Sabbath than a man. Jesus showed them that God's Sabbath law surely does not forbid helping people and the "work" necessary to help someone. Helping is good. Not helping is bad. It pleased Jesus to help people. It displeased Him when the Pharisees would deny a man with a withered hand, or a crippled woman the help that only God could give.

Belief pleased Jesus, and He responded with favor, praise, healing, and deliverance. Disbelief displeased Jesus, and He responded with rebuke, grief, and could not heal where He was doubted.

Death displeased Jesus, and thus He was indignant and wept at the tomb of Lazarus, gripped with compassion for a mother who lost her only son. Jesus did not hide these emotions, yet in our culture those who have lost loved one can barely take off work or shed a tear. They are exhorted to "be strong." Who was, or is, or ever will be stronger than our Lord Jesus? Yet He cried for Lazarus and Mary and Martha, even knowing and intending to raise Lazarus from the dead. Tears from others caused Him compassion, not aggravation. God feels pleasure or displeasure, joy or grief, satisfaction or dissatisfaction, anger and regret. But He knows what He feels and why He feels it, and He speaks and acts upon these feelings in truth, righteousness, love and justice.

The Spirit in us is grieved when we speak untrue and unedifying words to each other.

Indeed, we can cause the Spirit grief.

I hope that we never do so again.

Now we come to lessons and principles in scripture that teach us how to be angry without sin as well as how to be pleased without sin.

Remember again, emotions have objects and we choose these objects according to God's word and will.

Solomon and Jesus agree in commanding men not to lust after women who are not their wives. These women should not be chosen as objects of visual/physical pleasure. God permits the man to desire his wife and to enjoy this desire. But to indulge this desire outside of marriage is sin. This emotion man can control indirectly by staying completely away from women who arouse sexual emotions, by "fleeing sexual immorality/youthful lust," by "not going near the door of her (the adulteress') house." So, we are to avoid objects of temptation, objects that arouse our desires against God's will, according to James, who tells us that the source of temptation is the enticement of our own desires. We control this. We control where we go and what we do and what we allow our eyes to see and our ears to hear. Where we do not have this control, we are not in sin. A man who drives and finds himself behind a scooter with a woman on it in a string bikini and no way to go around her or to pull over is not sinning. He is being tempted. But he is not sinning. (I have literally had this happen to me.) But what this man chooses to do with his thoughts or memory of this woman is up to him. He can indulge the memory of her body or deny himself the pleasure of this memory in the form of fantasy. How does he do this? By simply declaring to God and Himself that He submits to God and resists the devil, and by choosing another object to focus his mind on; perhaps beautiful praise and worship music that he enjoys listening to, perhaps even thinking of the beauty of his own wife, if he is married, and thanking God for her. God always makes a way of escape when one is tempted so that one can bear the temptation.

So, fleeing temptation, objects of temptation, and places of temptation is the way to control pleasing emotions that are against God's will; the way to hate sin and even the pleasures of sin. I have also found that thinking of the eternal consequences of sin makes it very easy to resist. I ask myself this question: is this attractive woman worth hell? No matter how much pleasure she may be able to give, even if she were 20 years old, vivacious and voluptuous, possibly maintaining physical beauty for 20 to 30 more years, perhaps even longer depending upon her health and heredity. Is 30 years worth of sexual pleasure comparable to an eternity in the lake of fire for this pleasure?

This is what Satan puts away from the mind. He focuses on the pleasure that the body must have right now!!

Now!!

The temporal physical pleasure, intense and insatiable, is what Satan focuses the tempted man or woman on. Whether physical intimacy for men or food for women, whether fantasy for men or romance novels for women, whether sports for men or shopping for women, this world focuses us on now and not forever. Therefore, by thinking of forever, the momentary pleasure becomes easy to resist. And the object of pleasure actually becomes an object of intense displeasure. The beautiful seductress becomes a mistress of Satan, loved by God of course and not my true enemy, but a servant of my enemy, like "the woman with the red dress on the matrix," a distraction, an idol, a goddess that seals my doom and opens the door to hell, the one who rows the boat to the lake of fire. Her kisses become the vessels of a sweet poison, a toxin, a potion for a spell that puts me into a deep blissful sleep, one that can only be awakened by the alarming screams of those in hell for the same reason. I see her as she is: an adulteress, a temptress, a seductress, and immoral and evil woman, because this is what scripture says. What does this woman need? Salvation and a husband. Therefore, I pray for her to be saved and married, and turn my eyes away from her. I do whatever it takes to avoid temptation, no matter how painful or inconvenient. This is what plucking out the eye and cutting of the hand mean. Note these actions: permanent, painful...final. I must burn all bridges to sin once and for all and forever. I must renounce all sinful objects of pleasure. This I have done and continue to prayerfully do. If you have not, this you must do as well.

Not only this, but you and I must renounce sinful anger. Sinful anger is anger without just cause and just response. Jesus tells us how to deal with one who has sinned against us or wronged us. So do James and Paul. I will start with Paul, move to James, and end with Jesus.

Paul says to be angry and do not sin or let the sun go down on our wrath, giving the devil an opportunity.

What is sin? It is a transgression of the law, according to John in his first epistle. It can be summarized in two commands:

Love God with all you heart and soul and mind and strength.
Love your neighbor as yourself, treating others as you want to
be treated, even your enemies.
Love God supremely.
Love people impartially.

Now, people sin when they love God with less than supreme love and when they don't treat others like they would want to be treated in the same situation.

Remember, we are told by Paul to not delight or take pleasure in iniquity (sin); to abhor evil and cling to what is good. Solomon said the fear of God is to hate evil. So it is safe to say that one should be angry if one knows for certain that God or man has been sinned against. The bold words are crucial. We will discuss this later.

Paul says to be displeased when God or man is sinned against, but don't sin against man (and thus against God) in your displeasure; in other words, as Paul said, do not return evil for evil. Do not be overcome by evil, but overcome evil with good. If someone sins against you, do not sin against him or her in return. Deal with this situation quickly and sinlessly.

James says to be quick to listen, slow to speak, and slow to wrath. He gives the reason for this, that the wrath of man does not produce the righteousness of God. So it is safe to assume that if one is quick to listen, slow to speak, and slow to wrath, man's wrath can produce the righteousness of God. This makes sense, because God has already declared Himself slow to anger. God is wonderful!! He does not command us to do what He Himself does not do. He doesn't just declare Himself slow to anger, He shows Himself to us as slow to anger in many examples.

I am an officer. Before one is convicted of a crime or rule violation in the jail, an investigation happens. What must be shown is that a rule has been violated and that the inmate sent to lockdown committed the violation. In a court of law, intent has to be proved. A person must knowingly and willingly transgress a law. Motive must be shown and proved through testimony or other evidence. My job gives me great respect for God being quick to listen, slow to speak, and slow to wrath.

Observe. God questions Adam and Eve, allowing them the opportunity to confess. The "rule" was broken knowingly and willingly. The "evidence" was the knowledge that Adam and Eve had of their nakedness, knowledge that God knew He did not give them. This is why God asked, "WHO TOLD YOU WERE NAKED? Did you eat from the tree that I commanded you not to eat from?" This question assumes that there were only two ways they could have found out they were naked: God or the forbidden tree.

Their answers reveal their crime. God, after listening, gives the judgment.

God warns Cain of his possible sin against Abel. When Cain disregards the warning and sins anyway, God still questions him first before rendering judgment, being quick to listen, slow to speak, and slow to wrath.

As we've seen, He delayed judging the earth for 120 years, having SEEN the thought and intentions of men and women being only evil all the time.

This next example gives me great respect for God. God comes down to earth in response to an outcry against Sodom and Gomorrah. He responds to this outcry! But He doesn't immediately take sides with those who cry out. Nor does He deny their cry. He goes down to see if the reality is as the out criers say. And if so, "I will KNOW" is what the all knowing says. This is beautiful! He investigated this situation thoroughly, listened to Abraham's intercession, and even gave Lot and his family a concession in terms of their destination. God was quick to listen to those who cried out to Him about Sodom and Gomorrah as well as to Abraham, and to Lot. He was slow to speak the command of judgment to the angels, and thus slow to express His wrath against the sins of Sodom and Gomorrah.

So, Paul tells us not to sin in our anger or let it continue longer than a day. James tells us to listen before we speak, delaying our speech and anger until we have heard the matter out fully. God give us the perfect example. Now Jesus gives us a very practical example of how to carry these principles out. Here is His example.

A member of the body sins against me, treating me in a way that he does not want to be treated. Let's make the sin specific: he lies on me, bearing false witness against his neighbor. Let's be even more specific. He tells my wife that I committed adultery against her with his wife.

According to Jesus, I am to first confront my brother alone, making known to him his sin. So I tell him that he lied on me concerning his wife and give him the evidence: that I have never been alone with her at any time or in any place, and that on the day the supposed adultery occurred I was with my wife and children at home, all day. The man refuses to repent.

Now, I take two or three witnesses, one being my wife, another being the deacon of the church, who visited me at the time the alleged adultery occurred, and finally the third being the deacon's wife, who was with him. We speak to him about this lie and want to know why he and his wife are promoting it. He refuses to believe us and insists that his wife would not lie about this.

Finally, the witnesses and I take the matter before the entire body of Christ. We tell the body what was said and all that has occurred until this meeting. The pastor and the body hear it. They question the man and woman, who both refuse to repent of their lie. So, now, according to Jesus, we are to discontinue fellowship with this couple until they repent. This is to be the expression of displeasure toward the brother and sister.

Note: the "punishment" is to fit the crime. But the church does all she can to be reconciled. This is the point of "turn the other cheek." It is a literal command concerning being insulted, as expressed in "back slapping" someone in the face. One is not to retaliate or focus on retaliation, allowing oneself to be disrespected once and even once again, not seeking revenge. Yet apply this command to what Jesus said about being sinned against. If a brother backslaps me, I am to confront him alone. If he refuses to repent, I am to bring two who witnessed the backslap. Not only does he not repent, he backslaps me again. So I bring two witnesses, one who saw the first back slap, and one who saw the second. If he still refuses to repent, the witnesses and I bring him to the church. If he will not repent after all of this, we disassociate ourselves from this person. Notice, throughout the entire "investigation," I did not backslap the man back. But also notice that I did not allow him to continue to hit me after it was clear that he had no intention to stop. The turn the other cheek command does not negate all the other commands God gave. God Himself gave the command of justice known as "eye for an eye and tooth for a tooth." God Himself said that if a man sheds blood, man should shed the murderer's blood. The issue is this: God is merciful and willing to forgive and pardon and wants us to be like Him. But He does not pardon forever, and He will not be taken lightly. This leads us to just responses to sin, or "righteous indignation."

In America there seem to be two extremes when it comes to emotions, specifically the emotion of anger. One is total suppression, masked as "coolness." The cool person expresses little to know emotions at all, unaffected, unbothered, unaroused, unangered.

The other extreme is the rage of the hulk, where anger and strength are viewed as power, combined with insanity and being "bitchy." "You don't want to mess with me," is the motto of this extreme.

Christians tend to go along with the cool extreme, believing that God Himself, since the cross, no longer gets angry, that He expressed all the anger that He has ever had or ever will have at the cross. If this were so, then why did He express anger at all before the cross? Surely God's patience would endure until the day of Jesus' death. Why did He get angry at all before? And why the judgments in the book of Revelations to those who are on earth? If all of His anger occurred on the cross, then why are there Hell and the Lake of Fire?

Surely God still gets angry, or there is no God!! This is the entire issue that some atheists have. They think that God watches all the atrocities and evils on earth with cold indifference. At most, He is "grieved." But never angry, because He is no longer the "vengeful Old Testament God." But the word of God says, "I, the Lord, do not change." Jesus is the same yesterday, today, and forever more. This means that God responds to evil the same way He did in the past. He hates evil just as He did before the cross, and He will hate it forever. But as we have seen, God's hatred of evil is not a merely seething passionate rage waiting to explode. God removes evil and replaces it with good, if man and woman want Him to. Jesus died so that you and I don't have to die. But if we refuse Christ, God's wrath remains. Indeed, Paul said that the wrath of God is revealed from heaven against sinful mankind. Paul did not say that it was revealed. He said that it IS revealed.

What are the parameters of anger?

Most of what we've already said gives the parameters. No matter how a person has wronged you, you have no excuse to sin against him or her.

You must rightly judge the situation, judging first whether the person has actually wronged you, then determining if the person even knows he or she has wronged you.

You must know whether he or she intended to wrong you. Third,

You must give them the opportunity to repent, being willing to totally forgive him or her.

After these things, if the person remains unrepentant, while interacting with them, before separating from them as Jesus said should happen, your must be in control of yourself, meaning what you say and how you say it; the content and character of your words.

Content means of course the actual words you say. Paul said:

Do not let ANY unwholesome talk come out of your mouth, but ONLY that which is helpful for building others up according to their needs; THAT IT MAY BENEFIT THOSE WHO LISTEN.

Your motivation must be edification and reconciliation, not punishment. So, as Paul again says, you must speak the truth in love.

The character of your words has to do with your volume and your tone of voice. Solomon says, "A soft word turns away wrath, but a harsh word stirs up anger." It is possible to say the right thing the wrong way. Sarcasm and negative attitude are examples of this. Much of American emotion is expressed in attitude and sarcasm, sometimes so subtle the "uninitiated" will not detect. By the uninitiated I mean the ones who don't know the games Americans play, the mind games, the double talk. This is sin, because our "yes" is not "yes" and our "no" is not "no." This kind of talk is from the evil one, who does not say what he means. Yelling is also unacceptable because it expresses a lack of self-control. Again, I do not write as one who has not fallen in this very way, but as one who seeks to not fall again.

However, having said this, I must make it clear that anger in tone can be expressed as long as it is not a substitute for direct and clear words of truth in love, and this anger can be expressed even while one is angry. In other words, if the angry person does want reconciliation, and is angry because of the breach in relationship caused by the offense, this anger is just and right and good and can be expressed.

I saw a "Jesus movie" where Jesus just could not wipe the smile off his face. Even when he said, "Get behind me Satan," to Peter, He was smiling. There are certain things that can't be genuinely said with a smile on the face, and I am sure that this is one of them. To smile while saying certain things is a contradiction, like expressing displeasure in words while expressing pleasure in facial expression.

I know with certainty that Jesus was never out of control. I also know that His "yes" was "yes" and His "no" was "no," that He didn't do "double talk" or deceptive sarcasm. But I know that He did become angry from the scriptures I quoted earlier. And I don't imagine His tone being soothing or a smile on His face. I imagine that He sounded displeased because He was displeased. We as Americans don't know what this looks like. We are not used to righteous expressions of anger. We are "outraged" at events on the news or in politics; "pissed off." In a sense, Americans love anger, as I said earlier, as a means of power and control. We love "the hulk." In our country we have "road rage" and "going 'postal.'" Think about it. When Americans talk about things that make them angry, they seem to fuel the flame of fury. Watch our movies and see. In many action movies with good guys and bad guys there comes the moment in the film where somebody just loses it. They "just can't take it any more." This is the part of the movie we wait for.

Rage.

Heavy metal music is full of rage. So is some rap. The crazy jealous woman who burns down the home of her cheating dog of a man is another depiction of this.

The anger of God is fiercer than the fiercest warrior's, and His scorn more to be feared than the scorn of woman. I believe we have all experienced righteous indignation and unrighteous indignation.

We are like God.

When our anger is like His, our conscience is clear and our words irresistible and irrefutable. When our anger is unlike His, we feel guilt, remorse, and shame in our conscience, and others either responds with more anger or cower in fear, but not the fear of the Lord. This cowering is not based upon the divine presence of righteousness, but rather the instability of the one who has lost all control and is dangerous. Yet this one is usually not respected at the time of the outburst of wrath. And this one usually doesn't respect him or herself at the time. But his or her pride will not allow him/her to relent or "back down." I know this feeling. I have been in this very ungodly state.

But I have also been "right." I have been angry without sin. Usually this righteous anger is after waiting and listening patiently, knowing that I have not disrespected the person who is sinning against me in word, deed, or attitude. In other words, I, in these situations, have loved this person as I loved myself, treating him or her as I wanted to be treated, AND I KNEW THAT I HAD DONE THIS. In other words, in this situation, I was blameless. Though blamelessness may be rare, it is possible, and we all have experienced at least one instance of it; a moment where we were right and we knew we were right. My late and beloved grandmother used to say that if a person was right, they could speak boldly, as long as they were right. I agree with her. So does the word of God.

When I have been right, so have my emotions and the expression of my emotions. Of course, this is the normal state of God our Father, and thus the source of His own freedom. Against the fruit of the Spirit there is no law, and one led by the Spirit is not subject to the law. On several occasions Moses expressed anger and seemed vindicated by God Himself, like when he broke the tablets of the 10 commandments, burned the golden calf, and made the Israelites drink the ashes from the calf. Or when he left Pharaoh in anger. But when he struck the rock in anger instead of speaking to it, God did not vindicate this anger, evidently because Moses misrepresented God, as though God were angry when He was not. Thus, righteous anger is the very anger of God, and we must fear not to misrepresent him.

Each position and function has its unique way to deal with the expression of anger against evil, which is some form of judgment.

As an officer, I can lock down inmates, write them a minor infraction warning, called a "ticket," remove them from their jobs, pepper spray them if they try to attack me, or send them back to their dorm or unit. In other words, I can enforce my commandments with them. Most of the time, if I am focused on the fact that I am a representative, I do not get angry. If they personally verbally attack me or insult me, I easily ignore this, usually because the insults are so foolish. But if they disrespect me as an officer, I am obligated to act. My "anger" can be assuaged by swift judgment.

As a father, I have been given the rod of discipline. I sometimes read Christian authors in parent books say don't "spank in anger." On one hand I understand them, on another they seem to think of all anger as bad and out of control. But I must say I understand their caution very much and respect it. Yet we are commanded to be angry but not sin, to hate evil and cling to good, and to bring our children up in the training and admonition o the Lord. I represent God the Father to my children. God says He is "slow to anger," not that He never angers. To "never anger" is unrealistic and ungodly. Yes, ungodly, because God does become angry; slowly, yes; but angry. I am to be like Him, slow to anger, gracious, merciful, compassionate, just. But I must also be holy and intolerant of defiance and rebellion, just as He is.

The key with children is making sure that they are not disciplined or spanked unless what they do is defiant and rebellious. Refrain from discipline in situations of immaturity or ignorance due to youth, or simply a misunderstanding from the parent's end. My wife is good at finding out why a situation happened. I am good at not hesitating. We need each other. When together, I believe it

good to let her investigate. Once she has done so, if she finds
guilt, I then enforce the law of God in our house, bringing
fear and trembling in relation to God. God is to be revered.
   Feared.
   This does not just mean "high respect and awe and
reverence." It means be afraid of his anger and His judgment
or discipline. Jesus Himself said God should be feared as the
one who could destroy both body and soul in hell. The
demons fear and tremble.
   So the rod is a legitimate expression of justice, discipline,
punishment, correction, and righteous indignation. We tend
to focus on correction/rehabilitation and not punishment.
But God does punish. This punishment is His justice and
righteousness towards those who refuse His grace, mercy,
compassion and patience, meant for repentance. So, the
governor has the "sword," (meaning a gun, pepper spay,
baton) and the father has the rod. Both give every
opportunity for repentance in loving patience. But if there is
no repentance, then they should be feared.
   The husband has his influence as the enforcement of his
authority over his wife. He does not have a sword, a rod, or a
fist with his wife. He instead has the sword of the Spirit,
which is the word of God. Christ said to one of the churches
in Asia that He would fight against her "with the sword of
His mouth," the sharp and two edged sword. He has his
love, his honor, and his word. If he commands and she rebels
in attitude and disobeys in action, he needs only to expose
this by the word of God, written or spoken. For example, he
could say, "Paul says in the epistle to Titus that women
should obey their husbands. I told you to do this and you did
not do it." That's all he needs to say. The Holy Spirit will do
the rest. I take again the example of how Jesus dealt with the
7 churches in Asia. Husbands are given no instructions for
"discipline." Therefore, I believe that the husband's loving
and truthful word are the enforcement of his authority. The

name of Christ is His badge. The word of Christ is His sword. If the woman rebels against the one who lays his life down for her, she misses out on the very love of Christ. By acting independently of her husband, she loses his blessing and covering and backing.

Peter warns the husband that if he mistreats his wife his prayers will go unheard; the doors of heaven close to him, God ignores Him. This is terrible! I don't want heaven closed to me or to be on God's bad side for mistreating my wife. But God does not love man more than woman nor woman more than man. He is just and impartial. So I feel it safe to assume that God will discontinue fellowship with the woman if she does not respect, submit to, and obey her husband. God closed the womb of Michal when she dishonored David. He opened the wombs of the Hebrew midwives when they honored Him. So God knows how to judge men and women according to how He made them. For now, I focus on how the husband is to express anger. He is to command his wife, and if she disobeys, he is to expose her disobedience and pray that God will deal with his wife until she repents and submits to him as the church does to Christ.

In the church, there is "excommunication," meaning the sinning saint is "banished" from fellowship so that the Spirit of God, and at times the devil, will deal with the "flesh" according to Paul. Judgment begins with the house of God. Saints were weak, sick, and dying in Corinth because they disrespected the Lord's body at the communion table.

Beware, children of God.

So if a brother angers you, or a sister in the Lord, do what Jesus said.

As you can see, anger issues are authority issues, because anger as an emotion is based upon frustration, or as a wise brother in the Lord said, a "blocked goal." With this, scripture agrees, for James says this:

Where do wars and fights come from among you? Do they not come from your desires for pleasure that war in your members? You lust and do not have. You murder and covet and cannot obtain. You fight and war. Yet you do not have because you do not ask. You ask and do not receive, because you ask amiss, that you may spend it on your pleasures. James 4:1-4

Desire
Pleasure
Having
Obtaining

Simply put, you want something that would bring you pleasure and you can't get it.

An issue of the will
An issue of authority

Usually anger is based upon the assumption of the right to have whatever you want.

Rights
Authority

But in America, "might makes right." In other words, if you can take it by fighting for it and winning the fight, you can have it. The strong should rule, and thus have what they want. But what do they want? Pleasure.

So, those who are in authority have a means to deal with anger, which is usually caused by some challenge of the God given right they have to rule, unless they are abusing their authority. The abuse of authority usually leads to the anger of those under authority. And how they are to deal with the anger that comes from being under the abusive authority is usually a cause of great suffering and frustration.

Again, from my job as an officer, I have learned a lot about authority, being in authority and being under authority. All of us are in one of these two states.

In authority = commanding, rewarding obedience, punishing disobedience

Under authority = being commanded, being rewarded, being punished

You, the one who is reading, are an employer or an employee. Both of these states are good. We must all know how to lead and follow, how to give and take orders.

To those who take orders, if you are commanded to do that which directly disagrees with God's word, chapter and verse, or with clear reasonable conscience, you are to respectfully disobey. Note the word respectfully. According to Paul in Romans chapter 13, all authority comes from God and is appointed by God. So you respect God's delegation and refuse disrespect it because God is its source. So what do you do with your anger if an authority abuses you?

There is always a "chain of command," meaning no one but God the Father is unaccountable. On the movie, "Saving Private Ryan," Tom Hank's character said, "Complaints go up, not down." This means that one under authority complains to one in authority. Lets apply this to each of the areas of life Paul mentions in his epistles.

The wife, if mistreated by her husband, if she cannot respectfully appeal to her husband, should go to Christ, her husband's head. This takes trust from the wife. Some Christian women "take matters into their own hands" because the "boss" or "manager" is "invisible." For example, if you go to a restaurant and are dissatisfied with the waiter, you can say, "Let me speak to your manager." Usually in America one continues to go up the chain of command until one gets the answer one wants. If one goes all the way up to the owner and gets nothing, then the case is closed, because there is no one else to appeal to, except, of course, God, who is above all. And this is what the wife is to do, because there is no one in the home higher in authority than her husband, no human. But Christ is above Him, for Paul said to the

Corinthians that the man is the head of the woman, Christ is the head of the man, and God is the head of Christ. God the Father is the highest authority, the Most High God. So, the woman can and should go to Christ if her husband mistreats her, and Christ will most assuredly deal with him. To the believing wives who read this, do you trust Christ? Do you trust him enough to continue to respect and submit to an unbelieving husband or a carnal husband? Christ is faithful and will protect you, provide for you, and vindicate you. In the case of physical abuse, you can respectfully appeal to the police, still respecting your husband and standing by him, even if you must stand by him from a distance, or in extreme cases, while he is in jail. You should not desire his imprisonment or embarrassment, but you should not allow him to physically hurt you or the children. But he is not to be treated as the enemy. This is a tragedy and must be seen as such.

Husbands you are to appeal to Christ as well after you have exposed any disrespect or disobedience. Even if your wife "provokes you," appeal to Christ and leave the house if you must. The sword of the Spirit enforces your authority, which is the word of God. Use the word, and the shield of faith to quench the fiery darts of provocation and disrespect. But trust Christ. And if you have a wife who hits and is dangerous, do all that you can to block her attacks, and if she won't stop, appeal to the same governmental authorities that she would. It is against the law for her to hit you as well, as I can fully bear witness to as an officer, who sees women in jail for physically striking their husbands as well. It is wrong for both the man and the woman to hit each other.

Children, if your father or mother is not a "good parent," still respect them and obey them, and appeal to God the Father for protection. If they are physically abusive, meaning you are a young adult, 13 and above, and fear that they will cause you permanent physical damage or death, appeal to authority, but don't do this lightly. Still honor them. But if it is clear that your life is in danger, you can appeal to child protective services or the police. I must say that even this can be abused, meaning the police or services are called as an attempt to get some parents in trouble for being parents. God does authorize parents to spank children, BUT NOT ADULTS. For practical purposes, I will define adult with a physical definition, the ability to have children. If your son can impregnate a woman, consider him a man in the context of spanking. If your daughter can become pregnant, consider her a woman. I am not saying that you must spank the boy right up until this point, nor the girl. In fact, the earlier spankings stop, the better, assuming you have done it skillfully, wisely, and lovingly from the time they were little children who knew right from wrong until they were young boys and girls, around the ages of 7. Ideally, it seems that spankings should end by the time they are 7, but I cannot guarantee this with scripture. But I can say that the rod in scripture, in relation to parents and discipline, seem to focus on children and not men and women. The unruly young adult child in the Law of Moses was stoned. Under the New covenant we do not do this, but God enforces the principle expressed in the Ten Commandments. Those who dishonor father and mother do not live out the fullness of their days. God brings this about, not us. So in summary, if your father "provokes you to wrath," as Paul forbids fathers to do, appeal to God the Father, or even to a godly mother, godly meaning respectful and submissive. This kind of mother will not disrespect your father or allow you to do so, but will hear you and help you compassionately. If the mother is ungodly and the father is godly, do the same, appeal to the godly father, who has authority over the mother and can protect you. If neither father nor mother is godly, appeal to any godly family member you have. If you have no godly family members, then appeal to godly friends or teachers. If you cannot find one godly person in your life, then appeal to God directly. I am now talking about unloving or unfair parents, not physically abusive parents, meaning those who viciously and fatally beat children and young adults. I am not talking about lovingly spanking a little child who is old enough to know and understand a parent's command and deliberately disobeys it, spanking hard enough to cause the child to cry, but not hard enough to permanently scar/bruise/injure the child, and of course, not hard enough to kill the child. The key word is child. Clearly when the son or daughter can bear children, they should not be spanked. But before this age, it is up to the parents and the state of the child. If spanking has been done effectively, the child should get fewer and fewer spankings the older they get, until, assuming their salvation or subjection, they need no more spankings. Clearly Paul assumes that elders can have their children in subjection, so much so that it is a requirement for men who want to be elders. How could Paul require this if it were not under the control of the father who wants to be an elder?

Employers, if you are mistreated, there are two options, depending on the situation. One, according to Peter, is that if you are being wrongfully mistreated, meaning you are doing your job skillfully and respectfully, and your boss simply does not like you and mistreats you, you are to take it patiently. This honors Christ. Two, even if you take it patiently, appeal to the chain of command, meaning to your bosses boss, if you can and it would be wise. But if your boss has no boss above him or her, no human boss, then appeal to God to vindicate you and deliver you.

In other words, in all cases, anger can be expressed to God fully. The psalms are full of expressions of anger in relation to oppression and mistreatment, and prayers for vindication and God's judgment on those who mistreat and won't repent. Pray without ceasing. Do not be anxious or worried about anything, but pray about everything, and God will give you peace that surpasses human understanding. God will avenge you, whether husband or wife or child or employer or employee, or minister or one ministered to.

However, assuming ceaseless prayer, I have also seen in scripture and life that God expects us to take the authority and responsibility He gave to us, and that we are to go through the channels on earth that He put in place, being the origin of authority on earth. So, you are to appeal to human chains of command fully. Children appeal to father or mother. Wives appeal to your husband first, and by appeal I don't mean nag or argue, but submissively seek to be in agreement with your husband. Don't think you can skip over your husband and go to Christ without ever respectfully approaching your husband. The same is true for children and all who are under authority. My sergeant would consider it very disrespectful if I went "over his head" before talking to him. Mothers consider it disrespectful if a child asks fathers to do something that they have already said no to. Assistant managers are disrespected when the general manager is approached instead of them. Follow the chain of command in your situation, all the way up to God the Father if you need to (not that Christ and the Father are ever in disagreement, or that Christ will not give a "satisfactory answer." When I say that you go all the way to the Father, I mean through Christ.) This is how you deal with your anger if you are under authority.

So, in conclusion, emotions are neither holy nor unholy in and of themselves, whether pleasure or displeasure. The issue is the object of the emotion, and God's authority in relation to that object. Love what God loves. Hate what God hates. Be pleased with what God is pleased with. Be displeased with what God is displeased with. And respond to both the way God does, according to truth, and motivated by love. God be with you in this. Amen.

Impatience

He could not wait, or would not wait. Why? How do I know that Pierre was impatient? I don't. I must define impatience and see if his actions match the definition.

To be impatient is to choose not to wait when waiting is necessary. I don't know if this definition is sufficient. I will look in a dictionary.

Impatient:

-Not patient; not accepting delay, opposition, pain, etc. with calm or patience.

-Restless in desire or expectation; eagerly desirous

-Unable to wait patiently or tolerate delay, restless.

-Not willing to wait or delay.

Dictionary.com

Was Pierre "unwilling" or "unable" to wait? How do I know? I would have to ask him and see from his answer.

Patience seems to me to assume a limit on time. It assumes a delay in something happening, which means something is supposed to happen. For example, my goal was to open the dayroom at 0730. But I did not tell Pierre this. If I had told him, and he was unwilling and unable to wait, though he had the ability to wait, meaning there was no emergency situation that would make it wrong for him to delay action, and I knew this, then I could say that Pierre was impatient. It was 0725 when Pierre entered. He would have to wait 5 minutes, though he intended his break to begin at 0725. He would have to endure a 5-minute delay. Could he endure five minutes? Or was it that could he not endure an indefinite time, seeing as how I did not give him a definite time? Should indefinite times be considered in the context of the virtue of patience?

It does not seem to me to be the case that patience assumes indefiniteness in time. Even God will not endure sin forever. The sinner's time will come to an end. Yet God is patient. He delays judgment and punishment.

For example, He waited 120 years, the time it took Noah to build the ark, before He destroyed all but Noah and his family and the animals with Noah's family. He endured the evil of earth for 120 years. He also was willing to endure the evil of Nineveh for 40 days. He endured Nebuchadnezzar's pride for a year. He endured the sin of Sodom and Gomorrah until He came down to see for Himself their sin, then spoke to Abraham, and finally got Lot out of the city. He even delayed with Adam and Eve and Cain. He delays now in judging the earth. God is patient, longsuffering. Love is patient, longsuffering. The fruit of the Spirit is patience. The flesh is impatient. It must have what it wants now. It cannot wait. It will not wait. It must eat now. It must have sex now. It must be comfortable NOW.

God is gracious and merciful, full of compassion and great in mercy; slow to anger and abounding is in steadfast love and faithfulness, willing to relent, and not willing that any should perish, but that all would come to repentance. Hallelujah! God is so good. His patience has been my salvation. Where would I be if God had not been patient with me? I should be in hell, awaiting the lake of fire. But God is patient.

How long should we endure evil?

Perhaps Jesus gives us a "timescale."

If a man sins against you, go to that man alone.

If that man will not repent, take a witness to him.

If he still refuses to repent, take him before the church.

If he will not repent before the church, treat him like "a tax collector/sinner," i.e., stop close relations with him until he admits his guilt and commits not to sin against you in this way again (he repents.)

It seems to me that the "three strikes and you're out" rule, a rule that even nonbelievers acknowledge, gives us a minimum time to be patient. Give the offender three opportunities to repent, being calm and not expressing anger, irritation, or aggravation during these three opportunities. If after three opportunities there is no repentance, then anger can be expressed, and distance can come about, or whatever the just response should be in the specific situation.

Be quick to listen, slow to speak, slow to wrath.

Quick.

Slow.

Slow.

Now of course there are situations in which you and I cannot rightly be "patient." If an attempted murder is being committed, we must do what is in our power to stop it right now. And we see in scripture that God was not "patient" with Annanias and Sapphira. Yes, Peter gave each of them one opportunity to confess. But they had one opportunity only.

This is a warning to heed.

Do not take God's patience for granted. He is patient so that you and I will repent. But we may have sinned our very last time, having come to the end, even the very end of the patience of God.

If you need to, repent now.

Stop sinning now.

Keep from sin by the Spirit, now.

Be certain of your situation with God, and be wise.

I pray this is so for you. Amen.

Perpetual Arousal

I used to be a slave of passion and desire. I worshipped marital intimacy. I worshipped fantasy.

Jesus set me free. He delivered me. In today's language, he undid my addiction.

For a while, I didn't let go of it, still wanting it. But now I am married to a beautiful woman who is my best friend, and I am one with her spirit, soul, and body. Notice this union. It is not just physical, because she is not just physical. This is the lie of perpetual arousal. I am beginning to hate it. I am beginning to hate the lie.

Every time I get a glimpse of a music video with a woman in little to no clothing, I start to feel two things. One is akin to the feeling of eating too much ice cream or candy. Another is anger.

Bothered.

The ice cream feeling is related to too much of a good thing, to imbalance. Surely these women, whom God blessed with beautiful voices, who have minds, emotions, and wills; who have spirits, are more than just physically attractive. In a world of "women's liberation," why this physical focus? Are women not free to be more than beings of physical beauty? Is it still 'socialization' that causes them to dress and undress? Must cleavage show? Must skirts and pants be tight? Can I not just listen to a woman sing beautifully, deeply, and intelligently, without any sensuality? And what about women in authority? Does she not have enough power over me without her physical beauty? Do we need to see the imprint of a man's private areas for him to command us? Would this not be considered offensive? Yet why is it not offensive to be visually assaulted by certain women's bodies daily, whether Christian or non-Christian?

I have had enough of ice cream.

And what of the assault to my will? Must I see a woman's body whether I want to see it or not? "But why do you think I am dressing for you? Can't I just enjoy the beauty of my own body?" a woman may say. If you were the center of your own reality, in your own universe, yes, you could just "enjoy your own body." But that is just the point. Your body is not your own. It is God's. And He, as Your Creator, has the right to tell you how you should display your beauty, and to whom.

"But what about the men who promote this, who want this, who reward this with attention and fame?" These men are obviously in sin. And if you agree with them by dressing seductively, you also are obviously in sin; you who allow this negative attention upon your body. Who are you? Are you a man's or a woman's or your own object of desire? Must you "flaunt it" because you've got it? But for how long will you have "it?" How long will you keep this physical beauty?

I just want to be able to interact with a woman who is not my wife on the spiritual and intellectual level alone. I do not want her body. I should not want her body. I don't want to "look but don't touch." I don't want to look or touch. I just want to see a woman as a sister if she is my age or slightly younger, a mother if she is older, and a daughter if she is significantly younger. But this is not so. Some women my age or slightly younger do not treat me as a brother. Even some married women do not respect their own husbands, who should have forsaken all others for them, and they should have forsaken all other eyes on their bodies for the eyes of their husbands. Do you, married woman want to know if "you've still 'got it'?" Ask your husband. Do you like it when he looks at other women, other men's wives and daughters and sisters and mothers? Then why do you let other men look at you, the wife who wears tight and revealing clothing? What if your husband does not give you the attention and affection that he should? What if he focuses on other women, on women who take of their clothes for money, or participate in explicit movies?

What if you just want his attention and affection and appreciation?

If this is so, I am very sorry. I pray that God will convict your husband so that he will no longer dishonor you and leave you unloved. But know that God saw when Leah was unloved and Rachel was loved, and He responded, and He will do the same for you. But you be faithful. Be angry, but do not sin against God and your husband by seeking the attention of other men.

And what if you like the attention of men, beyond your husband? Repent. You are in sin. You make yourself an idol.

What if you like the "power of seduction?" Repent. You are in sin. You suffer from deception. As Jesus said to Pilate, you have no power except the power God gives and the power that man, made in his image, gives to you. Indeed. Men give you power. If they chose to ignore you, they could, and they would. You, the seductress, could walk naked into a room of some men watching the Super Bowl and the possible response you would receive would be anger or irritation. They would at least want you to wait until half time. I say this from watching some men who watch football, and seeing some women trying to get their attention. Usually women who seduce want the men to focus on them with the same intensity and tunnel vision that they focus on the game. I am not saying this focus on football is right. As a matter of fact, football/sports can also be an idol. But one idol is no better than another. Repent. Seek God's holy attention, and seek to help men to focus on God and not on you.

Do my words offend you, the woman who seduces men, who is "simply dressing in style?" Why? Why is it offensive for me to not want to see your body if you are not my wife, to want to know you as intelligent, deep, one with God? Would you rather me lust after you? To "resist" looking at your cleavage or waist in your low cut pants?

To the woman who does not practice seduction, who gives off NO sexuality, God and godly men praise you, because you are not a source of temptation. You honor your husband on earth, and your Husband in heaven. You are a true woman, your beauty is not fleeting and your charm is not deceitful. You are real.

You do not arouse desires that you have no intention to fulfill. You do not tease and taunt and act innocent, as though you have no idea what you are doing. You are true. You are my sister, my mother, and my daughter. You are like God, pointing me to the true and living God and not to yourself. You honor me, you honor my wife, and you honor my children. You are not a destroyer of homes and marriages and families. You lead to heaven, and not to hell. Your husband can trust you. God can trust you. You are like Mary, the mother of Jesus, and not like Eve, or Jezebel, or Herodias.

If you are a seductress, God does love you and will forgive you, just as Jesus forgave prostitutes and women who committed adultery. Not only does God love you, but I love you as well. I just want to see you as you are and forever will be, which is seen in your spirit and not your body. I love you and God loves you. But you must admit your sin, if you practice seduction. You must no longer play the victim, blaming men for your sin. God holds you responsible for what you wear, what you do with your body. Stop wearing it. Stop doing it. Give your body to God and to one man alone, your husband.

If you are still offended, know that you are offensive to God and godly men if you practice seduction. Do not be prideful. Humble yourself. Admit that you are wrong for defrauding, for arousing and tempting men with no desire to fulfill them; that you present yourself to them in a way that only a wife should present herself to her husband.

Men are the glory of God.
Women are the glory of men.
Therefore, women are the glory of God's glory.
This is the word of God concerning us both.
Be what God says you are, and in this way, be truly
Beautiful,
Inside and out,
Now and forever.

Amen.

The Praiseworthy Woman

"Charm is deceitful and beauty is vain, But a woman who fears the LORD, she shall be praised." Proverbs 31

Vain: transitory, unsatisfactory; leads astray
Deceitful: an untruth; by implication, a sham; to cheat, i.e. be untrue (usually in words) -- fail, deal falsely, lie.
Charm: a power of pleasing or attracting, as through personality or beauty
Beauty: the quality present in a thing or person that gives intense pleasure or deep satisfaction to the mind, whether arising from sensory manifestations (as shape, color, sound, etc.), a meaningful design or pattern, or something else (as a personality in which high spiritual qualities are manifest). **Dictionary.com**

A woman with the power to please or attract through her personality or physical beauty only is untrue; a cheat; a sham; she fails to ultimately please; she deals falsely; she lies. For this charm does not acknowledge God as the only true source of eternal pleasure.

The quality present in a woman's body or soul that gives intense pleasure or deep satisfaction to the mind, imagination, sensation or emotion, is transitory, unsatisfactory, temporary, leading one astray. For her body changes every day, and will not look young and new always.

But a woman, who reveres the Lord shines, should be commended, boasted about, and celebrated. This reverence is truly charming and eternally beautiful, inside and out.

She wears a coat of color,
Loved by some, feared by others, she's immortalized
In young men's eyes
Lust she breeds in the eyes of brothers

Violent sons make bitter mothers
So close your eyes, here's your surprise
The Beautiful is empty
The Beautiful is free
The Beautiful loves no one
The Beautiful stripped me
Words from a song by the former music group Creed

Who is God?
Who am I?
Who is she?
Who is my enemy?

God is my Creator and Father and Savior, the Creator and definer of marriage, man and woman, husband and wife.

I am a son of God, a creation.
He owns me as my Creator and redeemer.
I was created by Him and for Him.
I am a husband, the husband of Gracious Light.

She, Ungracious Darkness, is a seductress, an adulteress, not my wife.
My enemy is the tempter, tempting me to commit adultery with ungracious darkness.

I live for God.
I am faithful to my wife.
I flee the adulteress.
I resist the tempter.
This is truth.
What should I see when I see the woman of immorality?
I should see what she is.
If she tempts me, she is a temptress.
If she seeks to seduce me, she is a seductress.
If she is immodest, she is an immoral woman.

If she, knowing me to be married, wants to give her my body, she is an adulteress.

I should not praise her beauty or charm, both transitory/temporary, both a lie.

I should praise my wife's fear of the Lord.

Indeed, according to the word of God, her body is to satisfy me at all times and I am to be intoxicated by her love always.

Perhaps her body and her love are not so transitory. And I know they are not a lie. They are mine. And they nourish my masculinity and my progeny, who will live for all eternity. She is real.

Yet even with this, I should edify her spirit and praise her spirit's oneness with God's Spirit above all other praises of her physical beauty.

What do I see?
Who is she?

I see beauty that will not be for eternity and in the present is not for me. She, the adulteress, is not my wife. I am not authorized by God to allow her to be an object of physical or soul desire.

Authority.
The Creator has a right to determine relationships.
I respect His right to do so.
The liar lies.
That is what he does.
Lies.
Deception is when the obvious is no longer obvious.
Obviously, I have one wife-Gracious Light.
Is she or is she not Gracious-Light?
If she is, I am free to desire her.
If she is not, I am not.

Who is she?
Whose is she?
From where does she come?
What is her name?

Is my body honest?
Is it truthful?
Is it reliable?

I believe that it is not.
It has no morals.
It has no conscience.

If it sees my wife, it is aroused.
If it sees the seductress, it is aroused.
If it sees the adulteress, it is aroused.
If it sees the temptress, the immoral woman, the evil woman, they all arouse it.
It does not discriminate.

Not only does it not differentiate, it desires them all. It desires whomever and whatever will give it pleasure.

It does not care about God.
It only cares for self.

Hear the enemy.
"You must 'be true to yourself."
Honesty of body

Yet as we have seen, my body's honesty is not discriminatory.
It made no vow, and makes no promises.
It seeks to be lord, god, ruler, and master.
It will submit to her, if she will be its insatiable pleasure.

"Flee youthful lusts."
"Flee sexual immorality."
"Keep your way far from the immoral woman,
And do not go near the door of her house."
"Joseph did not consent to lie with Potiphar's wife or to be with her."

Why run?
Why flee?
Why not resist?

How can I resist myself?
How can I resist the blessing, "Be fruitful and multiply.
Fill the earth and subdue it?"

This is the treachery of the enemy.

Adultery
Idolatry
Paul said greed is idolatry.
Therefore adultery is greed. Obviously.

What does the adulteress offer that the wife does not?
Really?
What response can she bring from the body that is unique
to her?
What does she have, physically that the wife does not?

Beauty?
Fullness or voluptuousness or shapeliness?
Softness?
Sweetness of scent?
Silkiness of voice?

What? More intelligence, sensitivity, agreeability? If she possessed more of all of these than the wife possessed, then what? Why did you marry her? Did you know her before the adulteress? Or did you know them both before the vow? If you knew her after meeting your bride, then what of justice and fairness? Of course the body is unfair, unjust, uncaring. But what of conscience? Does it have a voice worth hearing? And if you knew them both, then why your wife and not the adulteress? Were you sober in judgment, knowing the untrustworthy nature of seduction's beauty, that she belongs to every man and yet no man?

Is your wife not beautiful?

Is she?

Is she?!

Who forced you to put the ring on her?

Who forced her to accept?

And you, adulteress wife, do not think you are unthought-of. Who is the adulterer that you "love." Who is he who unleashes your "passion?" Is he willing to forsake his wife? Does he commit to you as your husband did? What do you want that your husband will not give?

And what if your husband or wife is not all that he or she could be or should be (or would be without you?) What about the promise? What was the promise?

This is truth: A woman who fears the Lord is eternal, true, and praiseworthy.

She is the true woman.

She is the model.

She is priceless, mysterious, and rare.

Any man who finds her finds God's favor.

If you seek a wife, seek the woman who fears God. She is beautiful, truly beautiful, inside and out.

And if you seek a husband, seek the husband who fears God. He is handsome, truly handsome, inside and out.

Our God and Creator made man and woman. He loves and cherishes their union, physically and spiritually. God loves us so much, and only wants us to find true joy in his original intention for men and women. Trust what he says about both, and be blessed. Amen.

Reflections on Corrections

Bent on discontent and conflict, he needs, desires, wants, and asks.
But what does he want?

What he does not and cannot have.

And what is that?

For all the universe and existence to revolve around him and him alone.

The convict
The criminal
The inmate

Weary

Worn

Tired

Exhausted

How long will I have to endure them?

The selfish become more so, as do the irresponsible.

For years they come, in and out and in and out and in and out.

Demanding.

Some even commanding.

Their "constitutional rights."

Rights

May I have a "request form?" Do you know when the nurse is coming? Do you know when canteen is coming? (Inmates may purchase things while in jail. What they purchase is called "canteen.") Can you call the nurse? Can you call canteen? Can I speak to the sergeant, lieutenant, captain, major, colonel, sheriff, mayor, governor, president?

At times I feel sorrow and pity
At others anger

At others amusement
But mostly irritation

Are these men? Are these women?

Surely this is not God's intention.

Surely this is a glimpse of hell, and the opposite of heaven.

What is the solution?

Where is their salvation?

Indeed, the Savior sets captives free.

Free

Whoever sins is a slave of sin.

Whom the son sets free is free indeed.

Sin
Selfishness
Slavery

The Son of God frees slaves of sin.
But how does He liberate?

First the command: Repent.
Then the act: Baptism

Those who believe the message do both.

What is the message?

Jesus died for our sins according to the scriptures.
He was buried.
He rose from the dead according to the scriptures.

The reality and responsibility of sin upon men and women is assumed. But some of these take no responsibility and seem to feel no remorse. They evade conviction, spiritual and situational. They seek loopholes in "the system," and the system seems to allow them this.   They are not being prepared for the Day of Judgment, when there will be no parole, bail, plea day, or probation. The judgment will be perfectly just and eternally final. They won't be able to plead insanity.

God sees.
God knows.
God will judge, unless they repent.

But if they don't believe in sin, then where is conviction?

With God all things are possible, even the conviction of sin to those who seem to have no shame or guilt.

Where is the light of the world?

If the light is darkness, then the blind lead the blind.

Judgment begins with the house of God.

Loitering

Definition:
-to linger aimlessly or as if aimless in or about a place: to loiter around the bus terminal.

-to move in a slow, idle manner, making purposeless stops in the course of a trip, journey, errand, etc.: to loiter on the way to work.

Dictionary.com

This is what I have seen: purposelessness opposes purpose by its mere existence.

This may seem obvious, but wait.

Have you noticed how a person who seems to be wandering aimlessly almost intuitively gets in your way? He or she is not focused on you at all, or anybody or anything else at the time.

Focus-less.

Yet this one, without even trying, manages to get right in the spot you need to be and stay there, doing nothing. "Excuse me," you say. This one seems to be clueless as to what the two words mean. Sometimes this person fails to even acknowledge you. Sometimes the person lingers longer, now very much ON PURPOSE, though they have no real purpose; you know it, and he or she knows it. When brought to consciousness of the purposeless nature of the action or inaction, he embraces being an obstacle; she stubbornly refuses to move.

Observe the very dirty homeless person who "chooses," out of all the other places to linger, the children's playground. By dirty, I mean the person who urinates on himself while sleeping on the bench the parents usually sit on to watch their children playing. Why this bench? Why this playground, or any other playground? And why must the parents leave with their children instead of him leaving? The parents have a purpose: to watch and protect their children. The children have a purpose: to play for exercise and growth in using their bodies. But what is the purpose of this one who sleeps on the bench?

I observe the inmates I work with. They seem to constantly be in transit, in between, doing more than one thing, starting activities while leaving others unfinished; stopping and talking without their full uniform on; standing on the top tier, talking, on their way to their cells. These men spend the day playing cards, watching TV, sleeping, on the phone, on the rec. yard playing basketball; loitering through life. One of the clues to a crime about to be committed is a person in a place where he or she has no obvious purpose in being there.

And what about children in the neighborhood after 9 pm, running and yelling; sitting on the corner? What purpose are they serving? How many times do I have to go to them and ask them to be quiet so my baby can sleep, or so I can get up in the morning and go to work? How many times do I have to ask them who their parents are or to call the police?

I believe every crime and every sin or transgression begins with forsaking one's God given purpose.

Think of this. Perhaps the mystery of perfection lies in simply doing what one was created to do, no more, nor less, nor other. This makes sinless ness easy, or at least easier. Look at the Ten Commandments as an example.

1.   In order to worship another god before Jehovah,
2.   Or create a graven image to worship; the Israelites would have to forsake God's call to Abraham, or

God's purpose in setting them free from Pharaoh,
which was to worship Him before all the nations.

3. And to take His name in vain would be to forsake
    their own name, for He is the God of Abraham, the
    God of Isaac, and the God of Jacob.
4. If they refused to trust Him and worked constantly,
    not keeping the Sabbath, they are back in slavery,
    working idly.
5. To Dishonor father and mother is to dishonor origin
    and destination.
6. To steal is to negate another's purpose or use of an
    instrument of purpose.
7. To commit adultery is to forsake husband, wife or
    children, leaving one's purpose as husband or wife,
    and father or mother, which is to be a provider,
    protector and nurturer.
8. To bear false witness is again to negate another's
    purpose by negating reality itself, which is expressed
    most fully in
9. Murder.
10. And to covet is to live for creation instead of the
    Creator, who created you for Himself.

Indeed, I believe judgment day itself will answer this
single question: Did I fulfill the purpose for which God made
me? Indeed, does God regret making me? He knows the
plans He has for us, plans for good and not evil, to give us a
future and a hope. We are His workmanship, His poetry, and
His masterpiece, created in union with Jesus to do good
works, which God prepared for us before hand.

What is the purpose for which God created us? He
predestined us in His foreknowledge to be conformed to the
likeness of His Son. This was His intent from the very
beginning, for He said:

"Let us make man in our image, according to our likeness."

In the image of God we are to rule the earth. But if we are not like him, then we negate our destiny. Therefore, everything we intend, think, say, and do should be for the purpose of being conformed to the likeness of Jesus. And every relationship we have should serve this purpose as well. You should help me to be like Christ, and I should help you to do the same.

Everything else is loitering.

146

Appendix I

Whenever you, the one reading, and I, the one writing, read a book or listen to a speaker, we read or listen with unquestioned assumptions. We come with a certain view or views of reality. We come with answers to these questions:

Who am I?

Where did I come from?

What is my purpose?

Indeed, there are some who do not have answers to these questions. But even the "seekers," if they can read these words, they have some ideas of their own about truth.

You have some idea of your own about truth. There is a reason you are reading what I am writing.

I don't know the reason. I don't know your assumptions. But I want you to know mine.

I believe the best books on Christian assumptions are:

- The Book of Romans, by Paul the Apostle
- Mere Christianity, by C.S. Lewis, and
- More than a Carpenter, by Josh McDowell

However, if you don't have these books, or have never read them, I offer you my version of the assumptions in these books; Christian assumptions as I understand them.

First, I will state assumptions that I first heard from a Christian "apologist" named Ravi Zacharias. An "apologist" is: one who explains the Christian faith, and deals with intellectual objections to the faith so that one may make an "informed decision" about Jesus, having their objections dealt with satisfactorily, and thus having their objections removed.

These assumptions are not Ravi Zacharias' individual assumptions or opinions, nor does he claim them to be. They are "philosophical assumptions," meaning those who have thought deeply and systematically about reality (philosophers) have put into words what we all know intuitively; unquestioned assumptions, what we all accept as true without necessarily thinking about it or even being conscious of it.

These assumptions are:

-existence
-identity
-non-contradiction
-exclusion

In other words,

You, the one who is now reading, exist.

You exist.

If you agree, we can move on.

If you disagree, then by you disagreeing YOU still prove the point.

Again, you exist.

You are you. (Identity)

You are not me. (Non-contradiction)

Therefore, in the context of the assumption of your existence and identity and my existence and identity, we are either dealing with you or we are dealing with me, but not both of us at the same time and in the same sense. (Exclusion)

Now, from here, we focus on the questions of world view, on the perspective of reality.

Who are you?

Where did you come from?

What is your purpose?

Or put another way, and adding other questions:

What is our origin as humans?

What has gone wrong in our experience?

How can it be made right?

Origin

Opposition

Salvation

In other words, we all want to know our origin, our purpose, the meaning of our lives.

We all want to know why the "evils" or "wrongs" or pains of our lives happen.

We all want to know how to "make things right."

We all want to know where we come from and where we are going.

We all want to know what happens after we die.

Some one may say, "You are 'wrong.' I don't care about these questions at all."

Well, this one cares enough to tell me I am wrong.

Some may not care enough to even declare me wrong.

But I believe everyone cares about something or someone, namely themselves and their own happiness. And in some way, this care relates to the ultimate questions and assumptions.

Well, as far as Christian assumptions go, here are the answers to the ultimate questions, the questions of origin, opposition, and salvation:

***First, a Christian assumes the existence and identity of God. We assume that a being exists who was not born and will not and cannot die. We assume that this being is "self-existent and self-sufficient," meaning "He" has life in and of Himself. We assume that He is unlike any other being or thing we have ever experienced; that He is perfectly unique, perfectly good, perfectly wise, and perfectly powerful; that He is unlimited by time, space, or any other limitation. He is incomprehensible unless He chooses to reveal Himself. We say "He" because there is one who revealed Him as such. I will get to that later.

*Christians assume that God created us for His satisfaction. (Our origin and reason for living)

*Our first parents rejected God their Creator and purpose, and in doing so affected their descendants and their world (us and our world.) Their rejection of God was separation from God. They became like two leaves fallen from a tree. The separation of a leaf from a tree is the leaf's death. Though a leaf on the ground may still be green, it is indeed dead. Some of us are green leaves (young,) some of us are brown leaves (old), and some have already crinkled and fallen apart (completely dead.) Like a baby born of a woman with a crack addiction, or a baby born of a woman with AIDS, we were spiritually "stillborn," meaning we came into this world in a state of separation from God; and with an inclination of self-centered self gratification. And we in our lives have agreed to this state by willfully living as though God does not exist, or as though there is obscurity or uncertainty in God's identity (Opposition).

*But God, in His love for us, did not want us to remain separate from Him. Yet this separation was and is "just" or "right" or "fair," meaning this:

A creature that knowingly and willingly rejects the Creator should die. A creature who tries to live on its own, or for its own will, commits the ultimate crime, treason, or sin.

God, the Creator, is by right of creation King, Ruler, Lord, and Master. Based upon our assumption of right and wrong, we assume that a perfectly good King would not allow evil to forever go unpunished. This is so with God.

Yet God, in His love, chose to take our punishment for us, on our behalf, in our place, so that we would not have to suffer and die for our rebellious intentions and actions towards Him and each other. (Salvation)

Christians believe that God is love, meaning that when God loves, He is simply being true to who He really is. Yet love assumes an object of love, or an object that is loved. And Christians believe that God exists in unique and mysterious relationship which has come to be called "The Trinity," which means a relationship of perfect and complete unity between three identities. The way I understand this beautiful mystery is this: Existence---Expression---Experience.

God is the Self-existent one; the One who simply Is. He is.

God eternally expresses Himself, and this expression is also a person.   The relationship between Existence and Expression is like the relationship between a father and a son who is just like his father in every way.

The Self-Existent one is God the Father.

The only perfect Expression of the Self- Existent One is God the Son.

I, the one writing, have a son. My son came from me. God the Son eternally comes from God the Father. This is a mystery. I cannot perfectly explain it, if it can be perfectly "explained" at all.

The physical union between me and my wife, the highest expression of our union and love, resulted in the beautiful children we have. These children are a "combination" of me and my wife, of my family and her family.

The Holy Spirit is the experience of the Father and the Son united.

How do I know these things?

Jesus, God the Son revealed them.

Jesus revealed these things.

The primary history we have of Jesus is the New Testament, specifically the four gospels, which are four "testimonies" of the life, death, resurrection, and ascension of Jesus of Nazareth, who lived on earth about 2000 years ago. This is where the book "More than a Carpenter" comes in.

The reason this book is so powerful to me is that it shows this truth:

The resurrection of Jesus is an actual historical fact.

The way McDowell shows this is by applying a test used by historians when dealing with historical documents and historical events. This method is called historiography. The premise is that scientific facts are tested differently from historical facts, since the scientific method assumes control, experimentation, and repetition. Because these three clearly do not apply to an event in history, or to a past event, another kind of validation or invalidation is necessary. Historiography is similar to the way a lawyer proves or attempts to prove a historical event, a crime. Now of course, science is used in the context of DNA, medical expert opinions, etc. But the actual event, the crime, cannot be proved or disproved by science. A scientist may prove that a persons DNA was present at the place of the crime, and this data may help a lawyer to convince a jury, but the scientist cannot "prove" the event or the intent of the accused.

The historical event we want to focus on is the resurrection of Jesus. The reason for this is that Jesus' said that the proof of who He was and what He said would be that He would die and rise from the dead the third day of his death.

Before we can deal with this claim, we have to deal with the recordings of this claim, the writings themselves, the Gospels. Gospel means "good news." Testaments have to do with a promise, which the bible refers to with the word covenant. The good news is the fulfillment of a promise made by God to a man named Abraham, the ancestor of the Jewish people. God promised that one of Abraham's descendants would be a blessing to every family and nation on earth.

Now God made this promise in one of the books of the bible called Genesis, which is Hebrew for "beginnings."

So, we must deal with this book called the Bible, which is really a collection of books. We have to deal with this book because it is the source of Christian assumptions.

There are 66 books in the bible, 39 in what is called the "Old Testament" or "The First Testament," and 27 books in the "New Testament" or the "Second Testament."

The books of the Old Testament can be divided into these kinds of literature:

History
Poetry
Prophecy

The books of the New Testament can be divided into these kinds of literature:

History
Epistles
Prophecy

This is my premise:

Jesus is the fulfillment of the Old and New Testaments, the main character of the Bible, the one whom the Bible is all about. In Him the entire Bible (and all reality) is explained and makes sense. If we understand Him, we understand the Bible, which is about Him. The New Testament is about His coming to earth, His death, and His resurrection and ascension. The New Testament explains and fulfills the Old because the New Testament is all about Jesus. Or put another way, the Old Testament declares: the Messiah is coming. The Gospels in the New Testament declares: the Messiah is here. And the book of Acts as well as the rest of the New Testament declares: the Messiah is coming again.

Christ has died!

Christ had risen!

Christ will come again!

The history of Jesus is the essence of the Bible. So, if His history can be established as accurately recorded and accurately witnessed, and if it can be shown from the testimony of the New Testament that He was and is whom He said He was and is, then everything He said and can be taken as actual, factual, and trustworthy; everything that He said about EVERYTHING can be trusted as absolute truth!

So here we go.

Historiography has three components:

1. Bibliography: the number of copies for a historical document, and the length of time between when it was written and the actual event. For example, on 9/11/01, there was a terrorist attack on America. That was 7 years ago. If four people wrote a testimony about that day three days after the event, and there were 10 hand written copies of each testimony, then these copies could be compared to each other for accuracy, and the length of time between the writing and the event, as well as the length of time between the event and the present date, are useful in establishing credibility in terms of the accuracy of the copies. However, it doesn't establish whether the four people are trustworthy witnesses. This leads to the second test of historiography.

2. Internal Evidence: This has to do with the witnesses themselves. What makes a good witness? A. Was he there; at the time and place of the event in question? B. Are her senses sound? C. Is his mind sound? D. Are her motives trustworthy? For example, if witness number one was in Macon, Georgia, and he testified as though he were in New York, his testimony is unreliable. But if he interviewed his cousin, who was in New York in one of the World Trade Center buildings, and his cousin is sound in his physical senses, mind, and motives, and if the one interviewing is sound in all of those ways, then the testimony is likely to be credible.

3. Finally, there is the external witness. That means that people out side of the actual event can attest to a

given fact; people who are likely to be unbiased or unattached to the situation. The 9/11 event was so tragic and global in its effects that it is a well established fact of history. I wasn't there, but I know where I was when I saw the news on television.

Josh McDowell used historiography to test the New Testament scriptures. He showed that the more than 5,000 copies written within a generation of the actual events give great credibility to the accuracy of the copies.

He also showed that the internal evidence was highly credible. Matthew was one of the 12 disciples (followers) of Christ, an eye witness of the resurrected Christ. Mark was a disciple of Peter, who was in Jesus' "inner circle" of disciples, and who also saw Christ raised. Luke was a disciple of Paul, who persecuted believers until He saw Christ rose from the dead and began to preach about the one whom he used to persecute. John was the "beloved disciple," Jesus' closest disciple, and also and eyewitness of the resurrected Savior. After Judas Iscariot, who was one of the 12 followers of Jesus, betrayed Jesus and committed suicide, the 11 remaining disciples saw Jesus over a 40 day period before He ascended into heaven. Paul said that more than 500 people saw Jesus at once. James and Jude, Jesus' brothers, who didn't believe in Him before the resurrection, believed in Him afterwards, James' being a witness of Christ raised from the dead.

In addition to all of this, we have the life and death of the apostles. The 11 were cowardly and selfish before the resurrection. After Christ rose, all devoted their entire lives to Christ, in spite of being persecuted and cast out of Jewish society. All but one died horrible deaths because they would not renounce Jesus as the Messiah raised from the dead. John the beloved died of natural causes, although historical tradition has it that his persecutors attempted to boil him alive, but he was completely unharmed in the oil and thus banished to the Isle of Patmos, from whence he wrote the book of Revelation.

There is also external evidence in writings of Josephus and from disciples of John, and other early church leaders, known as "church fathers."

So, that is my partial summary of what Josh McDowell taught in "More than a Carpenter."

From C.S. Lewis' "Mere Christianity," we see the assumption of the Moral law, meaning that everyone deep down inside knows intuitively that there is a right and wrong. He said that these two truths are the foundation of all clear thinking about ourselves and the universe we live in:

We know the moral law.

We break the moral law.

Lewis shows that the source of the moral law is not instinct, but the standard by which we judge, express, and suppress instincts. It is not a social convention, but the standard by which we judge societies. It is not a mere convenience to social relations, but can be quite inconvenient.

It does not have its source in the universe, so it must have its source outside of the universe. After this he goes into "religions," and what the different religions teach about the moral law, and whether their teachings fit reality as we experience.

He showed that Atheism, which says there is no absolute truth or morality, clearly doesn't fit reality. He then shows that all religions basically fit into either Pantheism, which believes that God is all and all is God, such that in God there really is no good or evil, but only perspective, and in which the universe is really more like God's body than a separate creation. He then discusses Monotheism, which believes that God is definitely separate from all of creation like an artist is separate from his or her art, and that God definitely distinguishes between good and evil, and that He loves love and He hates hate. Muslims, Jews, and Christians are monotheists, and Hindus are Pantheists. Lewis then says that all other religions are either versions of Theism or Hinduism; that Islam is Christian heresy and Buddhism is Hindu heresy. He discusses a "life force" belief system where the universe is personified enough to where a sentimental person can enjoy a sunset and yet not have to deal with the "troublesome God of the Bible." And finally there is dualism, which believes that there is a real good deity and a real evil deity at war with each other. Lewis believed that other than Christianity, this belief system came closest to reality. Yet for there to be a real good deity and a real evil deity, there must be a standard outside of them both by which we know one is really good or really evil. He shows that evil is merely perverted good, and that for something to be "really good" and not just what we happen to like, it must be in agreement with the moral law, which can be summed up in the "golden rule:" treat others as you want to be treated.

What Lewis ultimately shows is that Christianity is the only belief system that accounts for all of the facts of our experience, and that "mere Christianity," the essence of what Christians believe is this: that Son of God became a man so that man might become a son of God. Man becomes a son of God through believing in whom Jesus is and what He did, that he died for our sins, rose from the dead, and lives forever as Our Lord and Savior. Lewis then shows the practical application of being God's children in this world.

Paul's letter to the Romans is, I believe, the best introduction to the faith and Christian assumption. And indeed, if I had to sum up what it means to be a believer, it can be summed up in one word:

BELIEVE!

Indeed, believers believe in Jesus, and as a result their sins are forgiven, since Jesus paid the penalty for sin, which is the death penalty. God, in His absolute perfection, perfectly hates all evil, from "great" evil to "small" evil. He cannot tolerate any evil or badness at all. All sin must be done away with in His presence. Jesus died so that we would not have to die. All that is necessary is for us to accept His death on our behalf, to believe in Him.

Once we believe, we are required to do one thing:

LOVE!

We love others as God has loved us. And how has God loved us? The motive of God's love can be summed up in one word:

GRACE!

Grace means unmerited or undeserved good will, meaning God loves us even though we don't deserve it. So we should love others, even when they don't deserve it.

God showed us mercy, meaning even though we deserved punishment, death and hell, He offers us life and heaven through accepting what Jesus did for us. Therefore, we should show mercy to those who do not deserve our good will, those who deserve to be punished for what they have done to us.

This does not mean God is no longer just. It means that God gives a person every opportunity to apologize for wrong doing and to stop doing it. If they refuse to admit wrong, apologize for it, put their trust in Jesus, and stop doing wrong, then God will punish them. In the same way, if a person refuses to stop doing wrong to us, then we should seek justice from God, but we should also ask God to help them to stop just as He did with us.

We love because God loved us.

Our love or doing good does not get us into heaven. We go to heaven by faith alone. But faith, as I say in one of the essays, is always expressed in love; loving people as we love ourselves, even loving our enemies; and loving God supremely, expressed in obedience to Him.

I just summed up the book of Romans; here it is in chapter form:

Romans 1-11: God declares a person righteous, or in a right relationship with Him because of faith in Jesus, and not by anything good they do to try to be a good person. BELIEVE

Romans 12-16 All commandments are summed up in one commandment: love your neighbor as your self. Love does not harm to a neighbor, therefore love is the fulfillment of the law. Therefore, each of us should seek to please his neighbor for his neighbor's good, leading him or her to encouragement in their faith in God. LOVE

So these are the assumptions of Christians, those who are "Christ like." I hope that you have believed in Jesus as a result of what you just read, if you were not a believer before.

159

Appendix II

I want to recap two things mentioned in the first appendix.

Testament: this word is related to the word "covenant," which is a promise or agreement between two persons or parties that cannot be cancelled once agreed upon. The first "testament" or covenant had to with the way man would approach God, which was through the Mosaic Law or system of sacrifices. This law and the sacrifices were not meant to bring people into relationship to God, which can only happen by faith, but rather the law and the ceremonies were to be a picture of what Jesus would do and fulfill. The second testament or covenant is the covenant that God fulfills in Jesus, which God made to Abraham concerning all the people on the earth. In this agreement, God accepts the sacrifice of Christ as the means of coming to Him, and not animal sacrifices. We only need believe in Jesus' death for us as the once and for all sacrifice for all sin, and we can then enter into the direct presence of God by His Spirit living in us, through believing in Jesus.

I said earlier that Christ revealed God as a Father, or a "He." This is why we say "He" when referring to God and not her. C.S. Lewis illustrates this truth shown in the Bible. God the Creator is not "male" but "masculine" in relation to creation. This is God the Father. God the Son became a man, a male, and is the Bridegroom, or Husband of believers, known as the church, which means those called out of this world into the new world to come, God's kingdom. God the Spirit is masculine in that He penetrates both men and women. Key word: penetration. So, masculinity pierces or penetrates. Femininity is pierced or penetrated. And here is the wonderful truth: God is so masculine, so piercing and penetrating, that all of creation, men and women, are feminine in relation to Him. Thus I am a "bride of Christ" though I am a man, and women are "sons of God" though women. Remember, this is all spiritual. These realities are spiritual. Women are pierced or penetrated by men, but the woman "penetrates" the baby with her breasts. So the masculine and the feminine are spiritual realities ultimately, and both pictures of God and Creation, or God's relation to the Son and the Spirit.

In conclusion, I urge you to read the Bible as a means to the end of knowing Jesus directly. At the end of the gospel of Luke I see two things that to me show the essence and truth of "Bible Study." First, I see Jesus walking and talking with two on a road called Emmaus. He "expounds" to them the things in the scripture concerning Himself. With the eleven, when He appears to them, He "opens their understanding so that they may comprehend the scriptures." Because of these two beautiful scenes, I pray this prayer when I read the scriptures:

"Spirit of the Lord Jesus Christ who is in me, please open my understanding so that I may comprehend the scriptures; and expound to me in all the scriptures the things concerning Yourself."

Unless Jesus does this, I don't believe we will come away from the scriptures comprehending them, comprehending the things concerning Jesus, the word embodied. What is the point of reading the Bible if it is not this? How can we, living 2000 years later in a different culture, with different paradigms, speaking a different language, understand the scriptures if those who lived in Jesus' day and were a part of the same culture and who spoke the same language could not comprehend?

I believe this is the source of our divisions and denominations: the teachings and interpretations of men and women instead of Christ Himself opening our understanding.

There were not 13 denominations and 13 interpretations of the scriptures when Jesus finished with the two on Emmaus Road and with the 11 disciples.   There were not 13 interpretations because there were not 13 messiahs.

One God and Father of all and in all who believe
One Lord
One Spirit
One Faith
One baptism

Because there is one Father, Son, and Spirit, and because faith comes by hearing the word of God, I state dogmatically my assumption concerning the scriptures: that there is one scripture, one Bible, no more and no less. The Lord who inspired His word is able to preserve His word.

May we be one as the Father and Son are one.
And may the world see our love and unity and know that we are indeed disciples of Jesus.
I long for this so much it brings me to tears as I write.
May we be the answer to Christ's prayer.
I love you, the one who reads.
If you want to respond to anything I have written, which I hope you do, please email me at this address:
honorcomesagain@live.com
God bless you.
Olatunde
The Return of Honor
Son of God
Brother of Jesus
Slave of the Spirit
A member of the Body of Christ
A faithful and true witness to the ends of the earth.
Perfectly pleasing in the sight of God for the Day of Judgment. Knowing this is so in the present.